ONLY
BELIEVE
for
HEALING

ONLY BELIEVE

for

HEALING

Smith WIGGLESWORTH

WHITAKER
HOUSE

ONLY BELIEVE FOR HEALING
90-Day Devotional

This book contains edited excerpts from *Smith Wigglesworth Devotional*, © 1999 by Whitaker House and *Smith Wigglesworth on Healing*, © 1999 by Whitaker House.

ISBN: 979-8-88769-015-5
eBook ISBN: 979-8-88769-016-2
Printed in the United States of America
© 2023 by Whitaker House

Whitaker House
1030 Hunt Valley Circle
New Kensington, PA 15068
www.whitakerhouse.com

Library of Congress Control Number: 2023936817

1 2 3 4 5 6 7 8 9 10 11 ⨆⨆ 30 29 28 27 26 25 24 23

CONTENTS

SECTION TWO: FAITH TO BELIEVE FOR HEALING

SECTION THREE: THE HOLY SPIRIT'S POWER TO HEAL

SECTION FOUR: JESUS'S NAME TO HEAL AND DELIVER

SECTION FIVE: GOD'S TRANSFORMING POWER

A DIVINE TOUCH

[The Lord] *heals all your diseases.*
—Psalm 103:3

Scripture reading: Psalm 103

One day, a stylishly dressed woman came to our meeting and on up to the platform. Under her arm, going down underneath her dress, was a crutch that nobody could see. She had been helpless in one leg for twenty years, had heard of what God was doing, and wanted to be prayed for. As soon as we prayed for her, she exclaimed, "What have you done with my leg?" Three times she asked, and then we saw that the crutch was loose and hanging and that she was standing straight up.

"We have done nothing with your leg. If anything has been done, it is God who has done it."

She answered, "I have been lame and used a crutch for twenty years, but my leg is perfect now."

We did not suggest that she kneel at the altar and thank God. However, she fell to her knees among the others and cried for God's mercy. I find that when God touches us, it is a divine touch of life and power. It thrills and quickens the body so that people know it is God. Then conviction comes, and they cry for mercy and salvation.

God heals today by the mighty power of His Word. However, the most important issue is, Do you know the Lord? Are you saved? Are you prepared to meet God? You may be an invalid as long as you live, but you may be saved by the power of God. You may have a strong, healthy body, but you may go straight to hell because you know nothing of the grace and salvation of God. Thank God I was saved in a moment, the moment I believed, and God will do the same for you.

God means by this divine power within you to have you follow the Word of God and the Spirit of God until you are entirely changed within. You might ask, "Wigglesworth, is there anything we can still ask God for in our body?" My answer is yes! I have a body in perfect condition, and I am sixty-five. Yet, it was not always so. This body was a frail, helpless body, but God fulfilled His Word to me: Jesus took my infirmities and my sicknesses, and by His stripes I am healed (Matthew 8:17; Isaiah 53:5).

Jesus took our infirmities. He bore our sicknesses; He came to heal our broken heartedness. Jesus wants us to come forth in divine likeness, in resurrection force, in the power of the Spirit, to walk in faith and understand His Word. That is what He meant when He said He would give us power over all the power of the enemy (Luke 10:19). Jesus will subdue all things until everything comes into perfect harmony with His will.

Is Jesus reigning over your affections, desires, and will? If so, when He reigns, you will be subject to His reigning power. He will be the authority over your whole life. When God reigns, everything must be subservient to His divine plan and will for us.

Thought for today: Praise God for anything that brings people to the throne of grace.

ONLY BELIEVE

Do not be afraid; only believe.
—Mark 5:36

Scripture reading: Mark 5:30–40

I want you to be full of enough joy to fill a deep well. If you have to make it happen, there is something wrong. If God makes it happen, there is always something right.

I have thought a great deal about momentum. When a train has arrived at a certain place, some people get out, but some go on to the end of the line. Let us go far enough with God. There is only one thing to do: stay fully aware and always be pressing on. It will not do to trust in the past. Let us go forward. When it comes to the power of momentum, the past will not do. We must have an inflow of the life of God manifested in us.

Only believe, only believe,
All things are possible, only believe.

The importance of that chorus is found in the word *only*. When you can get rid of yourself and everything else you rely on and have *only* God behind you, then you have reached a place of great reinforcement. If you help yourself—to the measure you help yourself—you will find that the life of God and the power of God are diminished.

Many people try to help themselves. What God wants is for us to cling to Him absolutely and entirely. This is the grand plan that God has for us: *"Only believe."* If we believe, we will have absolute rest and perfect submission.

Conditions on God's side are always beyond your asking or thinking. The conditions on your side cannot reach the other side unless you come into a place where you will rest on the omnipotent plan of God; then His plan cannot fail to be successful. *"Only believe"* and you will have absolute rest and perfect tranquility. You can then say, "God has said it, and it cannot fail." All His promises are *"Yes"* and *"Amen"* to those who believe (2 Corinthians 1:20).

Some have never tasted the grace of God, have never had the rest of God. Unbelief robs them of these blessings. It is possible to hear and yet not to perceive the truth. It is possible to read the Word and not share in the life it brings. It is necessary for us to have the Holy Spirit to unfold the Word and bring to us the life that is Christ. We can never fully understand the wonders of this redemption until we are full of the Holy Spirit.

Thought for today: Allow God to take absolute charge of your life. *Only believe.*

I AM THE LORD WHO HEALS

Is anyone among you sick? Let him call for the elders of the church, and let them pray over him, anointing him with oil in the name of the Lord. And the prayer of faith will save the sick, and the Lord will raise him up. And if he has committed sins, he will be forgiven.
—James 5:14–15

Scripture reading: James 5:7–20

We have in this precious Word a real basis for the truth of healing. In these verses, God gives very definite instructions to the sick. If you are sick, your part is to call for the elders of the church; it is their part to anoint and pray for you in faith. Then the whole situation rests with the Lord. When you have been anointed and prayed for, you can rest assured that the Lord will raise you up. It is the Word of God.

I believe that we all can see that the church cannot play with this business. If believers turn away from these clear instructions, they are in a place of tremendous danger. Those who refuse to obey do so to their unspeakable loss. Many turn away from the Lord like King Asa, who *"in his disease… did not seek the LORD"* (2 Chronicles 16:12). Consequently, *"he died"* (v. 13).

Does the Lord meet those who look to Him for healing and who obey the instructions set forth in the book of James? Most assuredly. He will undertake for the most extreme case.

A woman came into one of my meetings suffering terribly. Her whole arm was filled with poison, and her blood was so diseased that it was certain to lead to her death. We rebuked the thing, and the next day she testified that she was without pain and had slept all night, a thing she had not done for two months. To God be all the praise! You will find that He will do this kind of thing all along.

There was a man who had cancer. Night and day he had morphine every ten minutes. I went to see him. He said, "I do not know how to believe God! Oh, if only I could believe. Oh, if only God would work a miracle." I placed my hand upon him in Jesus's name. I said to the nurse, "You go to the other room. God will work a miracle."

The Spirit of God came upon me. In the name of Jesus, I laid hold of the evil power, with hatred in my heart against the power of Satan. While I was praying, this man was healed. I said to the nurse, "Come in." She did not understand what had happened, but the man knew that God had done it.

Previously, this man had had a hobby; it was yachting. He had been very fond of his yacht; it had been all he had wanted to talk about. Did he want to talk about yachting now? No! He said, "Tell me about Jesus—the Sin-Bearer—the Lamb of God."

He who made things happen—will you let Him in? God provides the double cure, for even if sin has been the cause of the sickness, His Word declares in James 5:15, *"If he has committed sins, he will be forgiven."*

Thought for today: If you turn away from any part of God's truth, the enemy will certainly get an advantage over you.

GOD KNOWS AND CAN HEAL

Jesus went about all the cities and villages, teaching in their syna-gogues, preaching the gospel of the kingdom, and healing every sick-ness and every disease among the people.
—Matthew 9:35

Scripture reading: Psalm 147

I was taken to see a beautiful nine-year-old boy who was lying on a bed. The mother and father were distraught because he had been lying there for months. They had to lift and feed him; he was like a statue with flashing eyes. As soon as I entered the place, the Lord revealed to me the cause of the trouble, so I said to the mother, "The Lord shows me there is something wrong with his stomach."

She said, "Oh no, we have had two physicians, and they say it is paralysis of the mind."

I said, "God reveals to me it is his stomach."

"Oh, no, it isn't. These physicians ought to know; they have X-rayed him."

The gentleman who brought me there said to the mother, "You have sent for this man; you have been the means of his coming; now don't you stand out against him. This man knows what he has got to do." So, I prayed over this boy and laid my hands on his stomach. He became sick, vomited a worm thirteen inches long, and was perfectly restored.

By the leading of the Holy Spirit, I knew what I needed to do, but Dr. Jesus knows more than that. He knows everything. All you have to do is call for Jesus, and He will come. Bless His name!

Jesus is with us. But has He come to you? He wants to come to you. He wants to share in your whole life. Truly, He wants to transform your life through His power right now. Oh, He is a precious Jesus! He is a lovely Savior! He is divine in all His attitudes toward us, and He makes our hearts burn. There is nothing like it.

Divine things are so much better than human things. Who will interfere with the divine mind of the Spirit that has all revelation, that understands the whole condition of life? The Word of God declares He knows all things (1 John 3:20) and is well acquainted with the manifestation of our bodies, for everything is naked and open before Him to whom we must give account (Hebrews 4:13).

Having the mind of the Spirit, we understand what the will of God is. When will we come into the knowledge of God? When we cease to rely on our own minds and allow ourselves to become clothed with the mind and authority of the mighty God.

Thought for today: Jesus saw every touch of the Father as a miracle, so we may expect to see miracles today.

JESUS AS HEALER

With men this is impossible, but with God all things are possible.
—Matthew 19:26

Scripture reading: Psalm 77

At one time, I had only a faint glimpse of Jesus as Healer. I was so bound that no human power could help me. My wife thought that I would pass away.

For six months, I had been suffering from appendicitis, occasionally getting temporary relief. I went to the mission where I was the pastor, but I fell to the floor in agony, and I was brought home to my bed. All night I was praying, pleading for deliverance, but none came. My wife was sure it was my call home to heaven and sent for a physician. He said that there was no possible chance for me—my body was too weak. Having had appendicitis for six months, my whole system was drained. He left my wife in a state of broken heartedness.

After he left, a young man and an old woman came to our door. I knew that she was a woman of real prayer. They came upstairs to my room. This young man jumped on the bed and commanded the evil spirit to come out of me. He shouted, "Come out, you devil! I command you to come out in the name of Jesus!" There was no chance for an argument or for me to tell him that I would never believe that there was a devil inside of me. The thing had to go in the name of Jesus, and it went. I was instantly healed.

I arose, dressed, and went downstairs. I was still in the plumbing business, and I asked my wife, "Is there any work in? I'm all right now, and I am going to work." There was a certain job to be done, and I picked up my tools and went off to do it. Just after I left, the doctor came in, put his hat down in the hall, and walked up to the bedroom. But the invalid was not there.

"Where is Mr. Wigglesworth?" he asked.

"Oh, doctor, he's gone out to work," said my wife.

"You'll never see him alive again," said the doctor. "They'll bring him back a corpse."

Well, God was not ready for me to be a corpse! Since that time, the Lord has given me the privilege of praying for people with appendicitis in many parts of the world, and I have seen a great many people up and dressed within a quarter of an hour from the time I prayed for them. We have a living Christ who is willing to meet people in every place.

Our God is real, and He has saving and healing power today. Our Jesus is just the same *"yesterday, today, and forever"* (Hebrews 13:8). He saves and heals today just as of old, and He wants to be your Savior and your Healer.

Thought for today: Oh, if you would only believe God! What would happen? The greatest things!

DEMONSTRATIONS OF GOD'S MIGHT

On this rock I will build My church, and the gates of Hades shall not prevail against it.
—Matthew 16:18

Scripture reading: Matthew 16:5–26

God is pleased when we stand on the Rock and believe that He is unchangeable. If you will dare to believe God, you can defy all the powers of evil. There have been times in my life when I have dared to believe Him and have had the most remarkable experiences.

One day I was traveling in a railway coach, and there were two people in the coach who were very sick, a mother and her daughter. I said to them, "Look, I've something in this bag that will cure every case in the world. It has never been known to fail." They became very interested, and I went on to tell them more and more about this remedy that had never failed to remove disease and sickness. At last, they summoned up the courage to ask for a dose. So I opened my bag, took out my Bible, and read them the verse that says, *"I am the Lord who heals you"* (Exodus 15:26).

God's Word never fails. He will always heal you if you dare to believe Him. Men are searching everywhere today for things with which they can heal themselves, and they ignore the fact that the Balm of Gilead is within easy reach. As I talked about this wonderful Physician, the faith of both mother and daughter went out toward Him, and He healed them both right on the train.

God has made His Word so precious that if I could not get another copy of it, I would not part with my Bible for all the world. There is life in the Word. There is power in it. I find Christ in it, and He is the One I need for spirit, soul, and body. It tells me of the power of His name and the power of His blood for cleansing. *"The young lions lack and suffer hunger; but those who seek the Lord shall not lack any good thing"* (Psalm 34:10).

Another person came and spoke haltingly, "What can you do for me? I have had sixteen operations and have had my eardrums taken out." I wrote the words, "God has not forgotten how to make eardrums." She was so deaf that I do not think she would have heard a cannon go off. I anointed her and prayed, asking the Lord to replace the eardrums. But afterward she remained as deaf as it was possible to be. However, she saw other people getting healed and rejoicing. Had *"God forgotten to be gracious"* (Psalm 77:9)? Wasn't His power just the same?

She came the next night and said, "I have come to believe God tonight." Take care that you do not come in any other way. I prayed for her again and commanded her ears to be loosed in the name of Jesus. She believed, and the moment she believed, she heard. She ran and jumped on a chair and began to preach. Later, I let a pin drop, and she heard it touch the floor. *"With God all things are possible"* (Matthew 19:26). God can heal the worst case.

Thought for today: Faith is an act; faith is a leap; faith jumps in; faith claims. Faith has an author, and faith's author is Jesus.

A REMARKABLE CATCH

Let us run with endurance the race that is set before us, looking unto
Jesus, the author and finisher of our faith.
—Hebrews 12:1–2

Scripture reading: Luke 5:1–11

Peole crowded around Jesus, so He sat in a boat and taught them in order that all might hear His words. Then Jesus said to Peter, *"Launch out into the deep and let down your nets for a catch"* (Luke 5:4). Peter answered, *"We have toiled all night and caught nothing"* (v. 5). Perhaps he was thinking, "Lord, You know nothing about fishing. Daytime is the wrong time to fish." But he said, *"Nevertheless at Your word I will let down the net"* (v. 5). I believe every fish in the lake tried to get into that net. They wanted to see Jesus. I must see Jesus.

Peter filled one ship, then another. Oh, what would happen if you lowered all the nets? Believe God! He says, *"Look to Me, and be saved"* (Isaiah 45:22). He says, *"Come to Me, all you who labor and are heavy laden, and I will give you rest"* (Matthew 11:28). He says, *"He who believes in Me has everlasting life"* (John 6:47). Believe! Oh, believe! It is the Word of God.

Peter saw the ship sinking. He looked around and saw Jesus. He fell down at Jesus's feet, saying, *"Depart from me, for I am a sinful man, O Lord!"* (Luke 5:8). He and all who were with him were astonished at the number of fish that they had caught. That spotless Lamb stood there, and Jesus said to Peter, *"Do not be afraid. From now on you will catch men"* (v. 10).

To see Jesus is to see a new way, to see all things differently. It means a new life and new plans. As we gaze at Him, we are satisfied; there is none like Him. Sin moves away.

Jesus was the express image of the Father (Hebrews 1:3). The Father could not be in the midst, so He clothed Jesus with a body as well as with eternal resources. The living Son of God—the Son of His love—came to us with understanding, ministering the breath of His Father. We encountered a life-giving Spirit. The moment we believed, we had a new nature, a new life. Jesus brings a wonderful word, a sweet influence. Men and women see love in His eyes and are convicted of sin in His presence.

Let us gather together unto Him. Let us move toward Him. He has all we need. He will fulfill the desires of our hearts, granting all our petitions, including the healing of our bodies and our souls.

Thought for today: God has no use for anyone who is not hungering and thirsting for even more of Him and His righteousness.

A VISION BECOMES REALITY

He Himself took our infirmities and bore our sicknesses.
—Matthew 8:17

Scripture reading: Isaiah 53:1–12

I want to tell you a remarkable story. One day I was standing at the bottom of Shanklin Road in Belfast, Ireland, with a piece of paper in my hand, looking at the addresses of where I had to go, when a man came over and said to me, "Are you visiting the sick?" "Yes," I said. "Go there," he said, and pointed to a house nearby.

I knocked at the door. No reply. I knocked again, and then a voice inside said, "Come in!" So I opened the door and walked in. Then a young man pointed for me to go up the stairway.

When I got up onto the landing, there was a door wide open. I walked right through the doorway and found a woman sitting up on the bed. As soon as I looked at her, I knew she couldn't speak to me, so I began to pray. She was rocking back and forth, gasping for breath. I knew she was beyond answering me.

When I prayed, the Lord said to me—the Holy Spirit said distinctly—"Read Isaiah 53." So, I opened the Book and began to read aloud,

Who has believed our report? And to whom has the arm of the LORD been revealed? For He shall grow up before Him as a tender plant, and as a root out of dry ground. (Isaiah 53:1–2)

When I got to the fifth verse, *"But He was wounded for our transgressions, He was bruised for our iniquities; the chastisement for our peace was upon Him, and by His stripes we are healed,"* the woman shouted, "I am healed!"

"Oh!" I said. "Tell me what happened."

"Two weeks ago, I was cleaning the house," she said. "In moving some furniture, I strained my heart. The doctors examined me and said that I would die of suffocation. But last night, in the middle of the night, I saw you come into the room. When you saw me, you knew I could not speak, so you began to pray. Then you opened to Isaiah 53 and read until you came to the fifth verse, and when you read the fifth verse, I was completely healed. That was a vision; now it is a fact!"

Now that is a word from the Lord! You will never get anything more distinct than that from the Lord. People miss the greatest plan of healing because of moving from one thing to another. Become grounded. I know the Word of God is still true. God wants you to take the Word, claim the Word, and believe the Word. That is the perfect way of healing. Do not turn to the right hand or to the left (Deuteronomy 5:32) but believe God.

God wants to sweep away all unbelief from your heart. He wants you to dare to believe His Word. It is the Word of the Spirit. If you allow anything to come between you and the Word, it will poison your whole system, and you will have no hope. It is like the devil putting a spear into you. The Word of Life is the breath of heaven, the life-giving power by which your very self is changed. By it, you begin to bear the image of the heavenly One.

Thought for today: One bit of unbelief against the Word is poison.

DAY 9

THE BREAD OF HEALING

If a son asks for bread from any father among you,
will he give him a stone?
—Luke 11:11

Scripture reading: Mark 7:24–30; Luke 11:5–13

The following question arises: Are salvation and healing for all? They are for all who will press right in and claim their portion. Do you remember the case of that Syro-Phoenician woman who wanted the demon cast out of her daughter? Jesus said to her, *"Let the children be filled first, for it is not good to take the children's bread and throw it to the little dogs"* (Mark 7:27). Note that healing and deliverance are here spoken of by the Master as *"the children's bread."* Therefore, if you are a child of God, you can surely press in for your portion.

The Syro-Phoenician woman purposed to get from the Lord what she was after, and she said, *"Yes, Lord, yet even the little dogs under the table eat from the children's crumbs"* (v. 28). Jesus was stirred as He saw the faith of this woman, and He told her, *"For this saying go your way; the demon has gone out of your daughter"* (v. 29).

Today many children of God are refusing their blood-purchased portion of health in Christ and throwing it away. Meanwhile, sinners are pressing through to Jesus and picking it up from under the table and are finding the cure, not only for their bodies, but also for their spirits and souls. The Syro-Phoenician woman went home and found that the demon had indeed gone out of her daughter. Today there is bread—there is life and health—for every child of God through His powerful Word.

The Word can drive every disease away from your body. Healing is your portion in Christ, who Himself is our bread, our life, our health, our

25

all in all. Though you may be deep in sin, you can come to Him in repentance, and He will forgive and cleanse and heal you. His words are spirit and life to those who will receive them (John 6:63). There is a promise in the last verse of Joel that says, "*I will cleanse their blood that I have not cleansed*" (Joel 3:21 KJV). This essentially says that He will provide new life within. The life of Jesus Christ, God's Son, can so purify people's hearts and minds that they become entirely transformed—spirit, soul, and body.

The sick people were around the pool of Bethesda, and one particular man had been there a long time. His infirmity was thirty-eight years' standing. Now and again an opportunity to be healed would come as the angel stirred the waters, but he would be sick at heart as he saw another step in and be healed before him. Then one day Jesus was passing that way, and seeing him lying there in that sad condition, He asked, "*Do you want to be made well?*" (John 5:6). Jesus said it, and His words are "*from everlasting to everlasting*" (Psalm 90:2). These are His words today to you, tried and tested one. You may say, like this poor sick man, "I have missed every opportunity until now." Never mind that. "*Do you want to be made well?*"

Thought for today: One touch of living faith in Jesus is all that is required for wholeness to be your portion.

HELP FOR THE HURTING

You, O Lord, are a God full of compassion, and gracious,
longsuffering and abundant in mercy and truth.
—Psalm 86:15

Scripture reading: Lamentations 3:21–41

In Sydney, Australia, a man with a cane passed by a friend and me. He had to get down and then twist over, and the torture on his face made a deep impression on my soul. I asked myself, "Is it right to pass by this man?" So I said to my friend, "There is a man in awful distress, and I cannot go farther. I must speak to him."

I went over to this man and said to him, "You seem to be in great trouble."

"Yes," he said, "I am no good and never will be."

I said, "You see that hotel? Be in front of that door in five minutes, and I will pray for you, and you will be able to stand as straight as any man here." This statement exercised my faith in Jesus.

I came back after paying a bill, and he was there. I will never forget how he wondered why a stranger would stop him on the street and tell him he would be made to stand straight. However, I had said it, so it had to be. Never say anything for bravado. Always be sure of your ground and be sure that you are honoring God. If there is anything about the situation that will make *you* special, it will bring you sorrow. Your whole ministry has to be along the lines of His grace and blessing.

We helped this man up the two steps, took him to the elevator, and got him upstairs. It was difficult to get him from the elevator to my room, as though Satan was making the last attempt for his life, but we got him there. In five minutes' time this man walked out of that room with his body as straight as any man's! He walked perfectly and declared he hadn't a pain in his body.

If God will stretch out His mighty power to loosen afflicted legs, what mercy will He extend to that soul of yours that must exist forever? He invites you: *"Come to Me, all you who labor and are heavy laden, and I will give you rest"* (Matthew 11:28).

God is willing, in His great mercy, to touch limbs with His mighty power, and if He is willing to do this, how much more eager He is to deliver from the power of Satan. How much more necessary it is for us to be healed of our soul sicknesses than of our bodily ailments! God is willing to give the double cure.

Thought for today: Grace is God's blessing coming down to you. You open the door to God as an act of faith, and God moves on your behalf.

"I CANNOT HELP BUT BELIEVE!"

But let him ask in faith, with no doubting, for he who doubts is like a wave of the sea driven and tossed by the wind.
—James 1:6

Scripture reading: James 1

Ayoung man in South Africa, who was dying of tuberculosis, read one of my books. He got saved, and then God healed him, and he became a pastor.

When I arrived in South Africa five years ago, he came up to me like a son to a father and said, "If you like, I will go with you all over South Africa." He bought the best car for the job. If you go to South Africa, you must have a car that can go through the plowed fields, one that will handle rough terrain and wet conditions. That young man drove me many miles through all the territories and God took us through everything.

Talk about life! Why, this is overcoming life!

When I arrived in Cape Town, a man was there whose deathly face was filled with the manifestation of cancer. I said to the people, "There is a man in this place suffering tremendously. He does not even know I am talking about him. I give you the choice. If you want me to deliver that man so that he can enjoy the meeting, I will go down in the name of the Lord and deliver him, or I will preach."

They answered me, "Come down." I went down, and the people saw what God can do. They saw that man shouting and raving, for he was like an intoxicated man. He was shouting, "I was bound, but I am free!" It was a wonderful thing to see that man changed and healed!

Another man we met, after spending a great deal of money on his wife for operation after operation, year after year, brought her helpless to the meeting. I went to her and said, "Look, this is the greatest opportunity of your life. I will give an altar call tonight. Fifty people will come up, and when you see them loosed, believe, and you will be loosed like them. Then we will have a testimony from you."

The people came up, and I laid my hands upon them in the name of the Lord. I said, "Testify of your healing," and they testified. This woman saw their faces, and when these people were through, I asked her, "Do you believe?" "I cannot help but believe!" she cried.

There is something in the manifestation of faith that stirs the soul. I laid my hands upon her in the name of Jesus, and the power of God went right through her. I said, "In the name of Jesus, arise and walk." And immediately, she walked.

An impossibility? If you dare the impossible, God will abundantly do far above all you ask or think (Ephesians 3:20).

Thought for today: If you do not venture out in faith, you remain ordinary as long as you live.

"I SEE JESUS!"

And the prayer of faith will save the sick,
and the Lord will raise him up.
—James 5:15

Scripture reading: Matthew 9:18–38

I was in Le Havre, France, and the power of God was being mightily manifested. A Greek man named Felix attended the meeting and became very zealous for God. He was very eager to get all he could to the meetings so that they could see that God was graciously visiting France. He found a certain bedridden woman who was paralyzed and could not move her arms or legs, and he told her about the Lord's healing at the meetings. He told her he would get me to come to her home if she wished.

She said, "My husband would never allow anyone who is not a Catholic to pray for me." She asked her husband to allow me to come and told him what Felix had told her about the power of God working in our midst. She reminded him, "You know that the doctors cannot help me, and the priests cannot help. Won't you let this man of God pray for me?" He finally consented, and I went to the house.

The simplicity of this woman and her childlike faith were beautiful to see. I showed her my oil bottle and said to her, "Here is oil. It is a symbol of the Holy Spirit. When that comes upon you, the Holy Spirit will begin to work, and the Lord will raise you up." God did something the moment the oil fell upon her. I looked toward the window, and I saw Jesus. (I have seen Him often. There is no painting that is a bit like Him; no artist can ever depict the beauty of my lovely Lord.)

The woman felt the power of God in her body and cried, "I'm free! My hands are free, my shoulders are free, and oh, I see Jesus! I'm free! I'm free!" The vision vanished, and the woman sat up in bed. Her legs were still bound, and I said to her, "I'll put my hands on your legs, and you will be free entirely."

As I put my hands on those legs covered with bedclothes, I looked and saw the Lord again. She saw Him, too, and cried, "He's there again. I'm free! I'm free!" She rose from her bed and walked around the room praising God, and we were all in tears as we saw His wonderful works. As we are told in James 5:15, "*The Lord will raise* [them] *up*" when the conditions are met.

Thought for today: Jesus Christ still has power to set the captives free.

THE LIVING WORD

When He had come down from the mountain, great multitudes followed Him. And behold, a leper came and worshiped Him, saying, "Lord, if You are willing, You can make me clean."
—Matthew 8:1–2

Scripture reading: Isaiah 53:1–11

When I read these words, my heart is moved, for I realize that Jesus is just as much present with us as He was in Jerusalem when He walked the earth. How it changes our whole nature as we comprehend what Jesus meant when He said, *"You search the Scriptures, for in them you think you have eternal life; and these are they which testify of Me"* (John 5:39).

This living Word is not given to us just because of the narratives or the wonderful parables that Jesus taught, but so that we, through it, might be changed. Beloved, His presence is so remarkable that if we will but call on Him, believing that He has the power to give eternal life at His command, we will be changed in body, soul, and spirit.

When Jesus was on earth and beheld suffering humanity, He was moved with compassion. He met the most difficult problems; one of the hardest conditions to meet was leprosy. The moment that leprosy was pronounced upon a person, it meant that he was doomed. Just as there was no remedy at that time for a leper, there is no earthly power that can deliver us from sin. Leprosy was the disease that had a death sentence, and sin means death to the spiritual man unless it is cleansed by the blood of Jesus.

Here was a leper with the seal of death on him, and there was only one hope. What was it? If he could come to Jesus, he would be healed. But how could a leper come to Jesus? When a leper came near other people, he had to cry out: *"Unclean! Unclean!"* (Leviticus 13:45)—so how could a leper ever get near to Jesus? The difficulty was tremendous, but when faith lays hold, impossibilities must yield.

When we touch the Divine and believe God, sins will be forgiven; diseases will go; circumstances will change. I can almost read the thoughts of the people as they passed by the leper: "You poor leper! If you had been where we were, you would have seen the most remarkable things happen, for people were delivered from all kinds of diseases today." The leper might have asked, "Where were you?" They would have answered, "We have been with Jesus!" Oh, the thrill of life when we have been with Jesus.

The leper, too, had come to see Jesus, but the eyes of the people were not on the leper now. They were watching for Jesus. When the leper cried out, "Unclean!" the crowd immediately moved away from him, leaving the path clear for the leper to be the first to get to Jesus. No one could turn him back.

No one can stop a man whose heart is set on reaching Jesus. No power on earth can stop a sinner from reaching the side of the Master if he has faith that will not be denied. Perhaps some have awful diseases in their bodies, or their souls are far away from God. They have been prayed for, and have prayed themselves, but the thing is not removed, and they are in the place where the leper was. He knew that Jesus could heal him. All he had to do was get close enough to Jesus, and He was made whole.

Thought for today: When you are in the place God wants you to be, you will be healed.

COME TO JESUS

Then Jesus put out His hand and touched him, saying, "I am willing; be cleansed." Immediately his leprosy was cleansed.
—Matthew 8:3

Scripture reading: Mark 1:28–45

Today there are many needy, afflicted people, but I do not think most of them are half as bad as this case that we just read of the leper in Matthew 8. There was no disease that was worse at the time. You may be suffering from tuberculosis, cancer, or other things, but God will show forth His perfect cleansing to you as well, His perfect healing, if you have a living faith in Christ. He is a wonderful Jesus.

This leper certainly would have been told about Jesus. So much is missed today because people are not constantly telling others what Jesus will do for them now. Someone had probably come to that leper and said, "Jesus can heal you." So he was filled with expectation as he saw the Lord coming down the mountainside. We understand that lepers were not allowed to come within reach of people; they were shut out as unclean. Ordinarily, it would have been very difficult for him to get near because of the crowd that surrounded Jesus. But as Jesus came down from the mountain, He met the leper; He came to the leper.

There was no help for him, humanly speaking, but nothing is too hard for Jesus. The man cried out, *"Lord, if You are willing, You can make me clean"* (Matthew 8:2). Was Jesus willing? You will find that He is always more willing to work than we are to give Him an opportunity to work. The trouble is that we do not come to Him; we do not ask Him for what He is more than willing to give.

If you are definite with Him, you will never go away disappointed. Divine life will flow into you, and instantaneously you will be delivered. Jesus makes one great sweeping statement from that day to this as He says, "I am willing; be cleansed." Immediately, the man's leprosy was cleansed.

Jesus is just the same today, and He says to you, "I am willing; be cleansed." He has an overflowing cup for you, a fullness of life. He will meet you in your absolute helplessness. Remember that Jesus told the distraught father, "If you can believe, all things are possible to him who believes" (Mark 9:23).

God has a real plan. It is very simple: come to Jesus. You will find Him just the same as He was in days of old (Hebrews 13:8).

Thought for today: You will never find Jesus missing an opportunity to do good.

GOD OPENS HIS STOREHOUSE

We never saw anything like this!
—Mark 2:12

Scripture reading: Matthew 14:14–20

If anything stirs me in my life, it is words such as these: "We never saw anything like this!"

These words were spoken following the healing of a paralyzed man. His four friends removed a portion of the roof in order to *"let down the bed on which the paralytic was lying"* (Mark 2:4). Jesus healed the man, and *"immediately he arose, took up the bed, and went out in the presence of them all"* (v. 12).

It is an ideal thing to get people to believe that when they ask, they will receive (Matthew 21:22). But how could it be otherwise? It must be so when God says it.

Now we have a beautiful word brought before us in the case of this paralyzed man, helpless and so weak that he could not help himself get to Jesus. Four men, whose hearts were full of compassion, carried the man to the house, but the house was full. Oh, I can see that house today as it was filled, jammed, and crammed. There was no room, even by the door. It was crowded inside and out.

Something should happen all the time to cause people to say, "We never saw anything like that." God is dissatisfied with stationary conditions. He opens the storehouse of the Most High, *"the unsearchable riches of Christ"* (Ephesians 3:8), to us. God wants to move us into this divine position so that we are completely new creations (2 Corinthians 5:17). You know that *"the flesh profits nothing"* (John 6:63). Paul says in Romans, *"The carnal mind is enmity against God; for it is not subject to the law of God, nor indeed can be"* (Romans 8:7).

As we cease to live in the old life and come to know the resurrection power of the Lord, we enter a place of rest, faith, joy, peace, blessing, and life everlasting. Glory to God!

May the Lord give us a new vision of Himself and fresh touches of divine life. May His presence shake off all that remains of the old life and bring us fully into His newness of life. May He reveal to us the greatness of His will concerning us, for there is no one who loves us like He does. Yes, beloved, there is no love like His, no compassion like His. He is filled with compassion and never fails to take those who will fully obey Him into the promised land.

Thought for today: So many people stop at the doorway when God, in His great plan, is inviting them into His treasury.

THE WAY TO JESUS

Come to Me, all you who labor and are heavy laden,
and I will give you rest.
—Matthew 11:28

Scripture reading: Matthew 7:13–27; 11:25–30

In God's Word, there is always more to follow, always more to know. If only we could be like children in taking in the mind of God, what wonderful things would happen. Do you apply the whole Bible to your life? It is grand. Never mind those who take only a part of it. You take it all! When we get such a thirst that nothing can satisfy us but God, we will have a royal time.

After the child of God comes into the sweetness of the perfume of the presence of God, he will have the hidden treasures of God. He will always be feeding on that blessed truth that will make life full of glory. Are you dry? There is no dry place in God, but all good things come out of hard times. The harder the place you are in, the more blessing can come out of it as you yield to His plan.

Oh, if only I had known God's plan in its fullness, I might never have had a tear in my life. God is so abundant, so full of love and mercy; there is no lack to those who trust in Him. I pray that God will give us a touch of reality, so that we may be able to trust Him all the way.

What an example of faith we have in the account of the paralytic's healing we just discussed. When the sick man's four friends found that the house where Jesus was staying was too crowded to enter, the men asked among themselves, "What will we do?" But there is always a way. I have never found faith to fail, never once. May the Holy Spirit give us a new touch of faith in God's unlimited power. May we have a living faith that will dare to trust Him and say, "Lord, I do believe."

There was no room, *"not even near the door"* (Mark 2:2), but these men said, "Let's go up on the roof." Unbelieving people would say, "Oh, that is silly, ridiculous, foolish!" But men of faith say, "We must get our friend help at all costs. It is nothing to move the roof. Let's go up and go through."

Lord, take us today, and let us go through; let us drop right into the arms of Jesus. It is a lovely place to drop into, out of your self-righteousness, out of your self-consciousness, out of your unbelief. Some people have been in a strange place of deadness for years, but God can shake them out of it. Thank God, some of the molds have been broken. It is a blessed thing when the old mold gets broken, for God has a new mold for us in Jesus.

Thought for today: God can perfect the imperfect by His own loving touch.

JESUS IS THE ONLY PLAN

The Son of Man has come to seek and to save that which was lost.
—Luke 19:10

Scripture reading: Mark 2:1–12

I tell you, friends, that since the day that Christ's blood was shed, since the day of His atonement, He has paid the price to meet all the world's needs and its cries of sorrow. Truly Jesus has met the needs of broken hearts and sorrowful spirits, withered limbs and broken bodies. God's dear Son paid the debt for all, for He *"took our infirmities and bore our sicknesses"* (Matthew 8:17). He was *"in all points tempted as we are, yet without sin"* (Hebrews 4:15).

I rejoice to bring Him to you today, even though it is in my crooked Yorkshire speech, and say to you that He is the only Jesus; He is the only plan; He is the only life; He is the only help. Thank God, He has triumphed to the utmost. He heals all who come to Him.

As the paralyzed man from Mark 2 was lowered through the roof to Jesus, there was a great commotion, and all the people gazed up at this strange sight. We read, *"When Jesus saw their faith, He said to the paralytic, 'Son, your sins are forgiven you'"* (Mark 2:5). What had the forgiveness of sins to do with the healing of this man? It had everything to do with it. Sin is at the root of disease. May the Lord cleanse us from outward sin and from inbred sin and take away all that hinders the power of God to work through us.

"Some of the scribes were sitting there and reasoning in their hearts" (v. 6). They asked, *"Who can forgive sins but God alone?"* (v. 7). But the Lord answered the thoughts of their hearts by saying:

Which is easier, to say to the paralytic, "Your sins are forgiven you," or to say, "Arise, take up your bed and walk"? But that you may know that the Son of Man has power on earth to forgive sins; He said to the paralytic, "I say to you, arise, take up your bed, and go to your house."

(Mark 2:9–11)

Jesus healed that man. He saw also the faith of the four friends. There is something in this for us today. Many people will not be saved unless some of you are used to stir them up. Remember that you are your *"brother's keeper"* (Genesis 4:9). When these men carried the paralyzed man, they pressed through until he could hear the voice of the Son of God, and liberty came to the captive. The man became strong by the power of God, arose, took up his bed, and went forth before them all.

I have seen wonderful things like this accomplished by the power of God. We must never think about our God in small ways. He spoke the Word one day and made the world. That is the kind of God we have, and He is just the same today. There is no change in Him. He is lovely and precious above all thought and comparison. There is none like Him.

Thought for today: We must take our brother to Jesus.

A GOD WHO ANSWERS

*Call to Me, and I will answer you, and show you great and mighty
things, which you do not know.*
—Jeremiah 33:3

Scripture reading: 1 John 5:14–15

I was in Long Beach, California, one day with a friend, and we were passing by a hotel. He told me of a doctor there who had a diseased leg. He had been suffering from it for six years and could not get around. We went up to his room and found four doctors there. "Well, doctor," I said, "I see you have plenty going on. I'll come again another day."

I was passing by his place another time, and the Spirit said, "Go see him." Poor doctor! He surely was in poor shape. He said, "I have been like this for six years, and nobody can help me." I said, "You need almighty God." People are trying to patch up their lives, but they cannot do anything without God. I talked to him for a while about the Lord and then prayed for him. I cried, "Come out of him in the name of Jesus." The doctor cried, "It is all gone!"

Oh, if we only knew Jesus! The trouble is getting people to believe Him. The simplicity of this salvation is so wonderful. His wholeness is to be your portion.

I was in Long Beach about six weeks later, and the sick were coming for prayer. Among those filling up the aisle was the doctor. I asked, "What is the trouble?" He answered, "Diabetes, but it will be all right tonight. I know it will be all right." There is no such thing as the Lord's not meeting your need. There are no *ifs* or *mays*; His promises are all *shalls*. *"All things are possible to him who believes"* (Mark 9:23). Oh, the name of Jesus! There is power in that name to meet every human need.

At that same meeting, there was an old man helping his son to the altar. He said, "He has fits—many every day." Then there was a woman with cancer. Oh, what sin has done! We read that when God brought forth His people from Egypt, *"there was not one feeble person among their tribes"* (Psalm 105:37 KJV). No disease! All healed by the power of God! I believe that God wants a people like that today.

I prayed for the woman who had the cancer, and she said, "I know I'm free! God has delivered me." Then they brought the boy with the fits, and I commanded the evil spirits to leave in the name of Jesus. Then I prayed for the doctor.

At the next night's meeting, the house was full. I called out, "Now, doctor, what about the diabetes?" He said, "It is gone." Then I said to the old man, "What about your son?" He said, "He hasn't had any fits since." We have a God who answers prayer!

Thought for today: One touch of Jesus's power meets the need of every crooked thing.

THE WONDERFUL PROMISES

[Through the] *exceedingly great and precious promises…you may be partakers of the divine nature.*
—2 Peter 1:4

Scripture reading: Philippians 3:1–15

The Lord has called us to share in His glory and power. As our faith claims His promises, we will see this truth evidenced. I remember one day I was holding a meeting. My uncle came to that meeting and said, "Aunt Mary would like to see you before she dies."

I went to see her, and she was assuredly dying. I said, "Lord, can't You do something?" All I did was stretch out my hands and lay them on her. It seemed as though there was an immediate touch of the glory and power of the Lord. Aunt Mary cried, "It is going all over my body." That day, she was made perfectly whole.

One day I was preaching, and a man brought a boy who was wrapped up in bandages. It was impossible for him to walk, so it was difficult for them to get him to the platform. They passed him over about six seats. The power of the Lord was present to heal, and it entered right into the child as I placed my hands on him. The child cried, "Daddy, it is going all over me." They took off the boy's bandages and found nothing wrong with him.

The Lord wants us to be walking letters of His Word. Jesus is the Word and is the power in us. It is His desire to work in and through us *"for His good pleasure"* (Philippians 2:13). We must believe that He is in us. There are boundless possibilities for us if we dare to act in God and dare to believe that the wonderful power of our living Christ will be made clear through us as we lay our hands on the sick in His name (Mark 16:18).

The Bible is the Word of God. It has the truths, and whatever people may say of them, they stand stationary, unmovable. Not one word of all His good promises will fail (1 Kings 8:56). His Word will come forth. In heaven it is settled (Psalm 119:89). On earth the fact must be made manifest that He is the God of everlasting power.

I feel the Holy Spirit is grieved with us when we know these things but do not do greater deeds for God. Does not the Holy Spirit show us wide-open doors of opportunity? Will we not let God lead us to greater things? Will we not believe God to take us on to greater demonstrations of His power?

Thought for today: Keep men's eyes off you but get their eyes on God and His Word.

EXPERIENCE RESURRECTION POWER

That I may know Him and the power of His resurrection,
and the fellowship of His sufferings.
—Philippians 3:10

Scripture reading: Philippians 3

Jesus had what Paul desired. Paul knew Jesus by revelation as we do. He did not know Him from being with Him in His human ministry as the other apostles did. Paul saw that Jesus lived in resurrection power. Paul wanted to gain the rest of faith, so he refused all hindrances and pressed on. He wanted to remove any interference that stood in the way of his knowing Christ.

One day, Jesus came upon a funeral procession. A widow's only son had died, and Jesus's great heart had compassion for her. He touched her son in his coffin and said, *"Young man, I say to you, arise"* (Luke 7:14). Death had no power; it could not hold him: *"He who was dead sat up and began to speak"* (v. 15). Oh, compassion is greater than death, greater than suffering. Oh, God, give it to us.

One day, I saw a woman with tumors. In the condition she was in, she could not live out that day. I said, "Do you want to live?" She could not speak, but she was able to move her finger. In the name of Jesus, I anointed her with oil. A man who was with me, said, "She's gone!"

It had been a little blind girl who had led me to this dying mother's bedside. Compassion broke my heart for that child. I had said to the mother, "Lift your finger." Carrying the mother across the room, I put her against the wardrobe. I held her there. I said, "In the name of Jesus, death, come out." Like a fallen tree, leaf after leaf, her body began moving. Upright instead of lifeless, her feet touched the floor. "In Jesus's name, walk," I said. She did, back to her bed.

I told this story in the service. There was a doctor there who said, "I'll prove that." He went to visit her and confirmed that the story was true. She told the doctor: "It is all true. I was in heaven, and I saw countless numbers. Then Jesus pointed, and I knew I had to go. Then I heard a voice saying, 'Walk, in the name of Jesus.'"

There is power in His resurrection. There is a *"righteousness which is from God by faith"* (Philippians 3:9). Are we able to comprehend it? Can we have it? It is His love. It is His life in us. It is His compassion.

See that you understand and possess the righteousness of God. Do not miss it. Oh, do not miss knowing Christ!

Thought for today: When the heart desires righteousness, God makes Himself known.

ARE YOU WILLING TO YIELD?

Now God worked unusual miracles by the hands of Paul.
—Acts 19:11

Scripture reading: Matthew 16:24–27; Luke 14:27–35

Paul had been putting many believers in prison, but God brought him to such a place of yieldedness and brokenness that he cried out, *"What do You want me to do?"* (Acts 9:6). Paul's choice was to be a bondservant for Jesus Christ.

Beloved, are you willing for God to have His way today? God said about Paul, *"I will show him how many things he must suffer for My name's sake"* (Acts 9:16). But Paul saw that these things were working out *"a far more exceeding and eternal weight of glory"* (2 Corinthians 4:17). Do you need a touch from God? Are you willing to follow Him? Will you obey Him?

When the prodigal son had returned and the father had killed the fatted calf and made a feast for him, the elder brother was angry and said, *"You never gave me a young goat, that I might make merry with my friends"* (Luke 15:29). But the father said to him, *"All that I have is yours"* (v. 31). He could kill a fatted calf at any time. When God can trust us, we will not come up short in anything.

"God worked unusual miracles by the hands of Paul." Let us notice the handkerchiefs that went from his body. This passage indicates that when Paul touched handkerchiefs and sent them forth, God worked special miracles through them: diseases departed from the sick, and evil spirits went out of them. Isn't this lovely? I believe that after we lay hands on these handkerchiefs and pray over them, they should be handled very sacredly. Even as we carry them, they will bring life, if we carry them in faith to

the suffering ones. The very effect, if you would only believe, would be to change your own body as you carry the handkerchief.

God wants to change our faith today. He wants us to see that it is not obtained by struggling and working and longing. *"The Father Himself loves you"* (John 16:27). *"He Himself took our infirmities and bore our sicknesses"* (Matthew 8:17). *"Come to Me, all you who labor and are heavy laden, and I will give you rest"* (Matthew 11:28).

Who is the man who will take the place of Paul and yield and yield and yield until God possesses him in such a way that power will flow from his body to the sick and suffering? It will have to be the power of Christ that flows. Don't think there is some magic power in the handkerchief, or you will miss the power. It is the living faith within the man who lays the handkerchief on his body, and the power of God through that faith. Praise God, we may lay hold of this living faith today. The blood has never lost its power. As we get in touch with Jesus, wonderful things will take place. And what else? We will get nearer and nearer to Him. Are you willing to yield?

Thought for today: Ministry always begins as soon as a person yields.

YIELD AND OBEY

Yield yourselves to the LORD.
—2 Chronicles 30:8

Scripture reading: John 15:1–14

Adear young Russian came to England. He did not know the language but learned it quickly and was mightily used and blessed by God. As the wonderful manifestations of the power of God were seen, people asked him the secret of his power, but he felt it was so sacred between him and God that he should not tell it.

When they pressed him a great deal, he finally said to them, "First, God called me, and His presence was so precious that I said to God at every call that I would obey Him. I yielded and yielded and yielded until I realized that I was simply clothed with another power altogether, and I realized that God had taken me—tongue, thoughts, and everything—and I was not myself, but it was Christ working through me."

Do you know that God has called you over and over and has put His hand upon you, but you have not yielded? Have you had the breathing of His power within you, calling you to prayer, and you have to confess that you have failed?

I went to a house one afternoon where I had been called, and I met a man at the door. He said, "My wife has not been out of bed for eight months; she is paralyzed. She has been looking forward so much to your coming. She is hoping God will raise her up." I went in and rebuked the devil's power. She said, "I know I am healed; if you leave, I will get up."

I left the house and went away, not hearing anything more about her. I went to a meeting that night, and a man jumped up and said he had something he wanted to say. He had to go to catch a train but wanted to talk first. He said, "I come to this city once a week, and I visit the sick all over the city. There is a woman I have been visiting, and I was very much distressed about her. She was paralyzed and lay on her bed for many months. However, when I went there today, she was up doing her work. God had healed her!"

I share this story because I want you to see Jesus. Yield to Him today.

Thought for today: If there are any *but*s in your attitude toward the Word of truth, there is something unyielded to the Spirit.

A GOD WHO SAVES

Then they cried out to the LORD in their trouble,
and He delivered them out of their distresses.
—Psalm 107:6

Scripture reading: Psalm 50

Does God know all about you? Is He acquainted with you altogether? Why should you, under any circumstances, believe that you will be better off by being diseased? When disease is impurity, why should you ever believe that you will be sanctified by having a great deal of sickness?

Some people talk about God being pleased to put disease on His children. "Here is a person I love," says God. "I will break his arm. Then so that he will love Me more, I will break his leg. So that he will love Me even more, I will give him a weak heart."

The whole thing won't stand daylight. It is not truth. Yet people are always talking this way, and they never think to read the Word of God, which says, *"Before I was afflicted I went astray"* (Psalm 119:67). They have never read the following words into their lives:

Fools, because of their transgression, and because of their iniquities, were afflicted. Their soul abhorred all manner of food, and they drew near to the gates of death. Then they cried out to the LORD in their trouble, and He saved them out of their distresses.

(Psalm 107:17–19)

Is it right to say, "You know, my brother, I have suffered so much in this affliction that it has made me know God better"? Well, now, before you agree, ask God for a lot more affliction so that you will get to know Him even better. If you won't ask for more affliction to make you still purer, I won't believe that the first affliction made you purer, because if it had, you would have more faith in it. It appears that you do not have faith in your afflictions. It is only talk, but talk doesn't count unless it is backed up by fact. However, if people can see that your words are backed up by fact, then they have some grounds for believing in them. The facts lie in the truth of the Word of God.

Christians need to understand the Word of God. We will become anemic and helpless without it. We are not any good for anything apart from the Word. It is everything. When the heavens and earth are melted away, then we will be as bright as the day because of the Word of God.

We know *"the word of God is quick, and powerful, and sharper than any twoedged sword, piercing even to the dividing asunder of soul and spirit, and of the joints and marrow, and is a discerner of the thoughts and intents of the heart"* (Hebrews 4:12 KJV). God's Word is like a sword piercing through. The Word is divinely appointed for us. Take it in; think it out; work it out. It is the truth.

Thought for today: Why not trust God, who knows all about you, instead of trusting in people who know only what you have told them?

DON'T GIVE SICKNESS A PLACE

For He shall give His angels charge over you,
to keep you in all your ways.
—Psalm 91:11

Scripture reading: Psalm 91

I have looked through my Bible, and I cannot find where God brings disease and sickness. I know it is the power of God that brings the glory. Yet it is the devil and not God at all who brings sickness and disease. Why does he? I know this: Satan is God's whip, and if you don't obey God, God will stand to one side, and Satan will attack you. But God will only allow him to attack so much, as was the case with Job. The Lord told Satan, "You may go only so far, and no further. Don't touch his life" (Job 2:6).

Why is Satan allowed to bring sickness? It is because we know better than we act. We give him the place to affect us. If we would be true to our convictions and walk according to the light we have been given, God would verify His presence in the midst of us, and we would know that sickness cannot *"come near [our] dwelling; for He shall give His angels charge over [us], to keep [us] in all [our] ways"* (Psalm 91:10–11).

When Satan can get to your body, he will, if possible, make the pain or the weakness so distracting that it will affect your mind and always bring your mind down to where the pain is. When that takes place, you do not have the same freedom in your spirit to lift up your heart and shout and praise the Lord. The distraction of the pain brings the foundational power, which ought to be full of praise to God, down into the body. And through that—concerning everybody who is afflicted—*"the kingdom of heaven suffers violence"* (Matthew 11:12).

Anything that takes me from a position where I am in an attitude of worship, peace, and joy, where I have a consciousness of the presence of God, where there is an inward moving of the powers of God that makes me able to lift myself up and live in the world as though I were not of it (because I am not of it)—anything that dethrones me from that attitude is evil. It is from the enemy.

The Psalms will keep you in an attitude of worship: *"I will extol You, my God, O King; and I will bless Your name forever and ever. Every day I will bless You, and I will praise Your name forever and ever"* (Psalm 145:1–3).

Thought for today: No one can say he wishes he were an overcomer but that he has failed and has no hope. Beloved, God can make you an overcomer.

TRANSFORMED BY GOD

Behold, I will do a new thing.
—Isaiah 43:19

Scripture reading: Titus 3

Thank God for His Word. Live it. Be moved by it.

When I was going to New Zealand and Australia, there were many to see me off. An Indian doctor rode in the same car with me to the docks and boarded the same ship. He was very quiet and took in all the things that were said on the ship. I began to preach, of course, and the Lord began to work among the people.

In the second class of the ship, there was a young man and his wife who were attendants for a lady and gentleman in the first class. As these two young people heard me talking to them privately and otherwise, they were very much impressed with God's love and power. Soon after, the lady they were attending got very sick. In her sickness and her loneliness, she could find no relief. They called in the doctor, and the doctor gave her no hope.

It was a strange dilemma for the sick woman was a well-known Christian Scientist; she had gone many places preaching this false doctrine. And yet, the young couple thought of me. Knowing the conditions and what she lived for, knowing that it was late in the day and that in the state of her mind, she could only receive the simplest word, I said to her, "Now you are very sick, and I won't talk to you about anything except this: I will pray for you in the name of Jesus Christ and the moment I pray, you will be healed."

And the moment I prayed, she was healed. That was *"like precious faith"* (2 Peter 1:1) in operation. After her healing, she became disturbed. I showed her the terrible state she was in and pointed out to her the folly and fallacy of her position. I showed her that there was nothing in Christian Science, that it is a lie from the beginning and an agency of hell. At best, it is a lie: preaching a lie and producing a lie.

Slowly, she came to her senses. She became so penitent and broken-hearted. But the thing that stirred her most was that she wanted to go preach the simple gospel of Christ wherever she had preached Christian Science. She asked me if she had to give up certain things. I won't mention the things; they are too vile. I said, "No, what you have to do is to see Jesus and take Jesus." When she saw the Lord in His purity, the other things had to go. At the presence of Jesus, all else goes.

This opened the door. I was asked to preach to all on the boat. This gave me a great opportunity. As I preached, the power of God fell, conviction came, and sinners were saved. They followed me into my cabin one after another. God was working powerfully there.

Then this Indian doctor came to me. He asked, "What will I do? Your preaching has changed me, but I must have a foundation. Will you spend some time with me?"

"Of course, I will."

Then we went alone to consider God's Word, and God broke the fallow ground. This Indian doctor decided to go right back home but as a new man. He had left a practice there. He told me of the great practice he had. He was going back to his practice to preach Jesus.

Thought for today: It is one thing to handle the Word of God; it is another thing to believe what God says.

GOD'S WONDER-WORKING POWER

Who can utter the mighty acts of the LORD?
Who can declare all His praise?
—Psalm 106:2

Scripture reading: Psalm 106

Aletter came to our house saying that a young man was very ill. He had been to our mission a few years before with a very bad foot. God had healed him that day.

Now, three years later, something else came upon him. His heart was failing, and he was helpless. He could not get up or dress or do anything for himself. In that condition, he asked his sister to write to me and see if I would pray. My wife said to go; she believed that God would give me that life. I went and when I arrived at this place, I found that the whole country was expecting that when I came, this man would be healed.

I said to the sister when I arrived, "I have come." "Yes," she said, "but it is too late." "Is he alive?" I asked. "Yes, barely alive," she said. I went in and put my hands on him and said, "Martin." He just breathed slightly and whispered, "The doctor said that if I move from this position, I will never move again." I said, "Do you know that the Scripture says, '*God is the strength of my heart and my portion forever*' (Psalm 73:26)"? He asked, "Should I get up?" I said, "No."

That day was spent in prayer and ministering the Word. I found a great state of unbelief in that house, but I saw that Martin had faith to be healed. God kept me there to pray for that place. I said to the family, "Get Martin's clothes ready; I believe he is to be raised up." I still felt the unbelief.

I went to the chapel and had prayer with several people there, and before noon they, too, believed that Martin would be healed. When I returned, I said, "Are his clothes ready?" They answered, "No." "Oh, will you hinder God's work in this house?" I exclaimed.

I walked into Martin's room alone. "Martin, I believe God will do a new thing today. I believe that when I lay hands on you, the glory of heaven will fill this place." I laid my hands on him in the name of the Father, Son, and Holy Spirit, and immediately the glory of the Lord filled the room, and I fell at once to the floor. I did not see what took place on the bed or in the room, but this young man began to shout, "Glory, glory!" and I heard him say, "For Your glory, Lord!" There he stood before me perfectly healed.

Martin went to the door and opened it, and his father stood there. "Father," he said, "the Lord has raised me up," and the father fell to the floor and cried for salvation.

God wants us to see that the power of the Holy Spirit coming upon people has something more in it than we have yet known. The power to heal and to baptize is available, but you must say, *"Lord, what do You want me to do?"* (Acts 9:6). If you had the eyes of Jesus, you would see that the harvest is already here (John 4:35). The Holy Spirit wants you for the purpose of manifesting Jesus through you. Oh, may you never be the same again!

Thought for today: The Holy Spirit moving upon us will make us to be like Him, and we will truly say, *"Lord, what do You want me to do?"*

THE FOUNDATION OF FAITH

In the beginning was the Word, and the Word was with God, and the Word was God. He was in the beginning with God. All things were made through Him, and without Him nothing was made that was made.
—John 1:1–3

Scripture reading: Luke 6:27–49

If we are ever going to make any progress in the divine life, we will have to have a real foundation. There is no foundation except the foundation of faith for us. All our actions and all that ever will come to us that is of any importance will be because we have a Rock. If you are on the Rock, no power can move you.

In any area or principle of your faith, you must have something established in you to bring it forth. There is no establishment outside God's Word. Everything else is sand. Everything else will break apart. If you build on anything else but the Word of God—on imaginations, sentimentality, or feelings—it will mean nothing without the foundation, and the foundation will have to be in the Word of God.

I was once on a train to Blackpool. It is a fashionable resort, and many people go there because of the high tides and the wonderful sights they see as the ocean surges up in massive mountains of sea. As I traveled, I looked over and said to a builder sitting near me, "Those men are building houses upon sand."

"Oh," he said, "you don't know. You are not a builder. Don't you know that we can pound that sand until it becomes like rock?"

"Nonsense!" I responded. I saw the argument was not going to profit, so I dropped it. By and by, we reached Blackpool, where the mountainous

61

waves come over. I saw a row of houses that had fallen flat, and drawing the attention of this man, I said, "Oh, look at those houses. See how flat they are." He forgot our previous conversation and said, "You know we have very large tides here, and these houses, being on the sand when the floods came, fell."

Our foundation of faith must be built on something better than sand, and everything is sand except the Word of God. There isn't anything else that will remain. We are told that heaven and earth will be melted with fervent heat (2 Peter 3:10). Yet we are told that the Word of God will be forever, and not one jot or tittle of the Word of God will fail (Matthew 5:18). If there is anything that satisfies me, it is in knowing that *"Your word is settled in heaven"* (Psalm 119:89). Another passage in Psalm 138:2 says, *"You have magnified Your word above all Your name."* The very establishment for me is the Word of God.

Here we have the foundation of all things, which is the Word. It is a substance; it is a power. It is a divine injunction to be born of this Word. God took the Word and made the world. Jesus, the Word of God, made it with the things that did not appear. And nothing has been made that has not been made by the Word (John 1:3). When we come to the truth of what that Word means, we will be able not only to build, but also to know; not only to know, but also to have. Live and operate in the substance of the Word. It is the foundation of our faith.

Thought for today: "Man shall not live by bread alone, but by every word of God" (Luke 4:4). Feast on the Word of God; discover its richness.

WHAT IS FAITH?

For in [the gospel of Christ] *the righteousness of God is revealed from faith to faith; as it is written, "The just shall live by faith."*
—Romans 1:17

Scripture reading: Romans 1:5–20

What is faith? It is the very nature of God. Faith is the Word of God. It is the personal inward flow of divine favor, which moves in every fiber of our being until our whole nature is so quickened that we live by faith, we move by faith, and we are going to be caught up to glory by faith! Faith is the glorious knowledge of a personal presence within you, changing you from strength to strength, from glory to glory, until you get to the place where you walk with God, and God thinks and speaks through you by the power of the Holy Spirit. Oh, it is grand; it is glorious!

God wants us to have far more than what we can handle and see, so He speaks of *"the substance of things hoped for, the evidence of things not seen"* (Hebrews 11:1). With the eye of faith, we may see the blessing in all its beauty and grandeur. God's Word is *"from everlasting to everlasting"* (Psalm 90:2), and *"faith is the substance"* (Hebrews 11:1).

If I would provide some man with wood, a saw, a hammer, and nails, he could produce a box. Why? Because he had the material. But God, without material, spoke the Word and produced this world with all its beauty. There was no material there, but the Word of God called it into being by His creative force. With the knowledge that you are born again by this incorruptible Word, which lives and abides forever (1 Peter 1:23), you know that within you is this living, definite hope, greater than yourself, more powerful than any dynamic force in the world, for faith works in you by the power of the new creation of God in Christ Jesus.

Therefore, with the audacity of faith, we should throw ourselves into the omnipotence of God's divine plan, for God has said to us, *"If you can believe, all things are possible to him who believes"* (Mark 9:23). It is possible for the power of God to be so manifest in your human life that you will never be as you were before; you will be always going forward from victory to victory, for faith knows no defeat.

The Word of God will bring you into a wonderful place of rest in faith. God intends for you to have a clear conception of what faith is, how faith came, and how it remains. Faith is in the divine plan, for it brings you to the open door so that you might enter in. You must have an open door, for you cannot open the door yourself. It is God who does it, but He wants you to be ready to step in and claim His promises of all the divine manifestations of power in the name of Christ Jesus. It is only then that you will be able to meet and conquer the enemy, for *"He who is in you is greater than he who is in the world"* (1 John 4:4).

Thought for today: Faith has power to make you what God wants you to be; only you must be ready to step into the plan and believe His Word.

A DIVINE FAITH

Have faith in God.
—Mark 11:22

Scripture reading: Psalm 9

There is a great difference between our faith and the faith of Jesus. Our faith comes to an end. Most people have come to the place where they have said, "Lord, I have gone so far; now I can go no further. I have used all the faith I have, and I just have to stop now and pray for more faith."

Thank God that we have the faith we do, but there is another faith. I remember one day being in northern England and visiting some sick people. I was taken to a house where a young woman was lying on her bed. Her reason had gone. Many things were manifested there that were satanic, and I knew it.

She was only a young woman, a beautiful child. Then the husband, a young man, came in with a baby, and he leaned over to kiss his wife. The moment he did, she threw herself onto the other side of the bed, just as a lunatic would do, with no consciousness of the presence of her husband. That was very heartbreaking. Then he took the baby and pressed the baby's lips to the mother. Again, she responded wildly. I said to a sister who was attending her, "Have you had anyone to help?"

"Oh," she said, "we have had everything."

But I said, "Have you no spiritual help?"

Her husband stormed out and said, "Help? You think that we believe God after we have had seven weeks of no sleep and of maniac conditions? You are mistaken. You have come to the wrong house."

That brought me to a place of compassion that something had to be done for this woman. With my faith, I began to penetrate the heavens with my prayers. I never saw anyone get anything from God who prayed with an earthly focus. If you receive anything from God, you will have to pray into heaven, for the answers are all there.

As I saw in the presence of God the limitations of my faith, there came another faith, a faith that could not be denied, a faith that took the promise, a faith that believed God's Word. And I came from that presence back again to earth, but I was not the same man under the same conditions that had confronted me before. In the name of Jesus, I was a man with a faith that could shake hell.

I said, "Come out of her in the name of Jesus!" She rolled over, fell asleep, and awakened fourteen hours later, perfectly sane and perfectly whole. Oh, there is faith, but Jesus wants to bring us all into a place in line with God where we cease to be, and His faith takes over. God must have the right of way, of thought and of purpose. God must have control.

Thought for today: You cannot know God by nature; you get to know Him by an open door of grace. The way to God is the way of faith; there isn't any other way.

AN UNWAVERING FAITH

Let us hold fast the confession of our hope without wavering,
for He who promised is faithful.
—Hebrews 10:23

Scripture reading: Hebrews 10:19–25

One day when I came home and found that my wife was out, I was told that she was down at Mitchell's. I had seen Mitchell earlier that day, and I knew that he was at the point of death. I knew that it would be impossible for him to survive the day unless the Lord undertook to heal him.

There are many who let up in sickness and do not take hold of the life of the Lord Jesus Christ that is provided for them. I hurried down to Mitchell's house, and as I got near, I heard terrible screams. I knew that something had happened. I saw Mrs. Mitchell on the staircase and asked, "What is up?" She replied, "He is gone! He is gone!"

I passed by her and went into the room. Immediately, I saw that Mitchell had passed away. I could not understand it, but I began to pray. My wife was always afraid that I would go too far, and she laid hold of me and said, "Don't, Dad! Don't you see that he is dead?" I continued to pray, and my wife continued to cry out to me, "Don't, Dad. Don't you see that he is dead?" But I continued praying.

I got as far as I could with my own faith, and then God laid hold of me. Oh, it was such a laying hold that I could believe for anything. The faith of the Lord Jesus laid hold of me, and a solid peace came into my heart. I shouted, "He lives! He lives! He lives!" And he is living today.

There is a difference between our faith and the faith of the Lord Jesus. The faith of the Lord Jesus is needed. Your faith may get to a place where it wavers. The faith of Christ never wavers. When you have His faith, the thing is finished. When you have that faith, you will never look at things as they are. You will see the things of nature give way to the things of the Spirit; you will see the temporal swallowed up in the eternal.

As we remain steadfast and unmovable on the ground of faith, we will see in perfect manifestation what we are believing the Lord to do.

Thought for today: It is when we are at the end of our own resources that we can enter into the riches of God's resources.

FAITH AT WORK

He…gave some to be apostles, some prophets, some evangelists,
and some pastors and teachers, for the equipping of the saints
for the work of ministry…till we all come to the unity of the faith
and of the knowledge of the Son of God.
—Ephesians 4:11–13

Scripture reading: Ephesians 4:7–5:1

A man traveled with me from Montreal to Vancouver and then on a ship to New Zealand. He was a dealer of racehorses. It seemed he could not leave me. He was frivolous and talked about races, but he could not keep up his end of the conversation. I did not struggle to keep my end up because mine is a living power. No person who has Jesus as the inward power of his body needs to tremble when Satan comes around. All he has to do is to *"stand still, and see the salvation of the* LORD*"* (Exodus 14:13).

This man entered into a good deal of frivolity and talk of this world. Coming upon a certain island of the Fiji group, we all disembarked, and God gave me wonderful liberty in preaching. The man came back afterwards; he did not go to meet his racing and card-playing chums. Instead, he came stealing back to the ship. With tears in his eyes, he said, "I am dying. I have been bitten by a snake." His skin had turned dark green, and his leg was swollen. "Can you help me?" he asked.

If we only knew the power of God! If we are in a place of substance, of reality, of ideal purpose, it is not human; we are dealing with almightiness. I have a present God. I have a living faith, and the living faith is the Word. The Word is life, and the Lord is *"the same yesterday, today, and forever"* (Hebrews 13:8). Placing my hands upon the serpent bite, I said, "In the name of Jesus, come out!" He looked at me, and the tears came. The swelling went down before his eyes, and he was perfect in a moment.

Yes, "*faith is the substance of things hoped for, the evidence of things not seen*" (Hebrews 11:1). Faith is what came into me when I believed. I was born of the incorruptible Word by the living virtue, life, and personality of God. I was instantly changed from nature to grace. I became a servant of God, and I became an enemy of unrighteousness.

The Holy Spirit wants us to clearly understand that we are a million times bigger than we know. Most Christians have no conception of what they are. Oh, that God would bring us into divine attractiveness by His almightiness so that all our bodies would wake up to resurrection force, to the divine, inward flow of eternal power coursing through our human frames. I believe God wants something to be in you that could never be unless you cease to live for yourself. God wants you to live for Him, to live for others. But, oh, to have the touch of God!

Thought for today: God wants us to be like the rising of the sun, filled with the rays of heaven, all the time beaming forth the gladness of the Spirit of the Almighty.

FAITH BASED ON KNOWLEDGE

For in it the righteousness of God is revealed from faith to faith;
as it is written, "The just shall live by faith."
—Romans 1:17

Scripture reading: Psalm 4

I was healed of appendicitis because of faith based on the knowledge of the experience of faith. When I have ministered to others, God has met and answered according to His will. We know that God will not fail us when we believe and trust in His power. The centurion had this faith when he said to Jesus, *"Speak a word, and my servant will be healed"* (Matthew 8:8). Jesus answered him, *"'Go your way; and as you have believed, so let it be done for you.' And his servant was healed that same hour"* (v. 13).

In one place where I was staying, a young man came in telling us that his sweetheart was dying; there was no hope. I said, "Only believe." This was faith based on knowledge. I knew that what God had done for me, He could do for her. We went to the house. Her sufferings were terrible to witness. I said, "In the name of Jesus, come out of her." She cried, "Mother, Mother, I am well." Then I said that the only way to make us believe it was for her to get up and dress. Soon she came down dressed. The doctor came in and examined her carefully. He said, "This is of God; this is the finger of God." It was faith based on knowledge.

If I were to receive a check for a thousand pounds and knew only imperfectly the character of the man who sent it, I would be careful of him. I would not rely on the money until the check was honored. Jesus, on the other hand, did great works because of His knowledge of His Father. He knew He could count on the character of God. Faith begets knowledge, fellowship, and communion. If you see imperfect faith, full of doubt, a wavering condition, it always comes because of imperfect knowledge.

At a meeting one evening, there was a seventy-seven-year-old woman who was paralyzed. She was there because of her faith to believe. The power of God came into her, and she was so strengthened and blessed after prayer that she rushed up and down in a marvelous way.

Brothers and sisters, what I see in this woman's healing is an illustration of what God will do. I am trusting that we will all be so strengthened today with the power of God that we will not allow any unbelief or fear to come into our hearts. On the contrary, we will know that we are created anew by a living faith and there is in that faith within us power to accomplish wonderful things for God.

Thought for today: God is more eager to answer than we are to ask.

THAT YOU BELIEVE IN HIM

"What shall we do, that we may work the works of God?"
Jesus answered and said to them, "This is the work of God,
that you believe in Him whom He sent."
—John 6:28–29

Scripture reading: Luke 9:1–11

I remember a person who had not been able to smell anything for four years. I said, "You will smell now if you believe." She went about smelling everything and was quite excited. The next day, she gave her testimony.

I was called to a hotel one day to pray for a man who had blood poisoning. I looked at his arm; it was very swollen. His arm, neck, and face were blue. He opened his eyes and said, "Can you save me? I am dying." I took hold of the arm and turned it round twice. It was an act of faith. I said, "In the name of Jesus, you are free." He swung his arm round and round and said, "Look! Jesus is that mighty, wonderful name, which God has said is greater than all." This same Jesus is the Deliverer of all humanity.

At another place, there was a man anointed with oil for a rupture. He came the next night and rose in the meeting saying, "This man is an impostor. He is deceiving the people. He told me last night I was healed; I am worse than ever today." I spoke to the evil power that held the man and rebuked it, telling the man he was indeed healed. He was a stonemason. The next day, he testified to lifting heavy weights and that God had met him. *"By His stripes we are healed....And the LORD has laid on Him the iniquity of us all"* (Isaiah 53:5–6). He was against the Word of God, not me.

"What shall we do, that we may work the works of God?" Jesus
answered and said to them, "This is the work of God, that you believe
in Him whom He sent." (John 6:28–29)

Anything else? Yes. He took our infirmities and healed all our diseases. I myself am a marvel of healing. If I fail to glorify God, the stones will cry out (Luke 19:37–40). Salvation is for all. Healing is for all. The baptism of the Holy Spirit is for all. Consider yourselves *"to be dead indeed to sin, but alive to God in Christ Jesus our Lord"* (Romans 6:11). By His grace, you will get the victory every time. It is possible to live a holy life.

Living faith brings glorious power and personality; it gives divine ability, for it is by faith that Christ is manifested in your mortal flesh by the Word of God. I do not want you to miss the knowledge that you have heard from God, and I want you to realize that God has changed you so that all weakness, fear, inability—everything that has made you a failure—has passed away.

Thought for today: The Holy Spirit has the latest news from the Godhead and has designed for us the right place at the right time.

FAITH IN THE VICTORY

This is the victory that has overcome the world; our faith.
—1 John 5:4

Scripture reading: 1 John 5:4–15

When I was ministering to the sick, a man came who was shriveled and weakened; his cheek bones were sticking out, his eyes sunken, and his neck all shriveled. He was just a form of a man. He whispered, for he could only speak with a weak voice, "Can you help me?"

I asked, "What is it?" He said he had had surgery to remove stomach cancer. As a result of the operation, he could not swallow.

He said, "I have tried to take some juice today, but it would not go down." He whispered, "I have a hole in my stomach. As I pour liquid in through a tube, my stomach receives that. I have been living this way for three months."

You could call it a shadow of life that he was living. Could I help him?

Look! This Book can help anybody. This Book is the essence of life. God moves as you believe. This Book is the Word of God. Every time I minister, every time I preach, I am impressed with the fact that the Word of God is full of life, full of vitality, and it changes us. God's Word must come to pass.

Could I help him? I said, "On the authority of this Word, this night you will have a big supper."

But he said he could not eat. "Do as I tell you," I answered.

"How can it be?"

"It is time," I said, "to go and eat a good supper." He went home and told his wife.

She could not understand it. She said, "You cannot eat. You cannot swallow."

But he whispered, "The man said I had to do it." He became hungry and ventured, "I will try it."

His wife prepared his supper. He took a mouthful, and it went down just as easily as possible. He went on eating food until he was full. The next morning, he was so full of joy because he had eaten again. He looked down out of curiosity to see the hole and found that God had closed it up!

But you ask, "Can He do it for me?" Yes, if you believe it. Let God have His way. Touch God now. Faith is the victory (1 John 5:4).

Thought for today: The Word of God is marrow to your bones. It is resurrection from every weakness; it is life from the dead.

BEGIN TO ACT

Be diligent to present yourself approved to God, a worker who does
not need to be ashamed, rightly dividing the word of truth.
—2 Timothy 2:15

Scripture reading: 2 Timothy 2:1–15; 20–21

God wants His glory to be seen. We are going to miss a great deal if we don't begin to act. But once we begin to act according to the will of God, we will find that God establishes our faith and from that day makes His promises real to us.

I was speaking one night about faith and what would take place if we believed God. When I left that place, it appeared that one man named Jack, who worked in the coal mine, had heard me. He had trouble with a stiff knee. A few days after the meeting, Jack said to his wife, "I cannot help but think every day that Wigglesworth's message was to stir us to do something. I cannot get away from it. All the men in the pit know how I walk with a stiff knee, and you know how you have wrapped it with yards of flannel. Well, I am going to act."

He got his wife to sit in front of him. "You have to be the congregation," he said. "I am going to act and do just as Wigglesworth did." He got hold of his leg unmercifully, saying, "Come out, you devils; come out in the name of Jesus! Now, Jesus, help me. Come out, you devils; come out." "Wife," he exclaimed, "they are gone! They are gone!"

Soon after, Jack went to his place of worship, and all the coal miners were there. As he told them his story, they became delighted and were filled with faith. They said, "Jack, come over here and help me." And Jack went. As soon as he was through in one home, he was invited to another, loosing these people from the pains they had gotten in the coal mine in Jesus's name.

We have no idea what God has for us if we will only begin to act! But, oh, the grace we need! If we do this work outside of Him, if we do it for ourselves, it will be a failure. We will be able to succeed only as we do the work in the name of Jesus. Oh, the love that God's Son can put into us if we are only humble enough, weak enough, and helpless enough to know that unless He does it, it will not be done!

Live and walk in the Spirit. Talk with God. Let go of what is earthly and take hold of God's ideals. God will bring you to an end of yourself. Begin with God this moment.

Thought for today: God wants us to be blessed, but first He wants us to be ready for the blessing.

EYES OF FAITH

Jesus went about…teaching…preaching…and healing.
—Matthew 4:23

Scripture reading: Isaiah 58:8–12

One day, a young woman from a place called Ramsbottom came to be healed of an enlargement of her thyroid gland. Before she came, she said, "I am going to be healed of this goiter, Mother." After one meeting, she came forward and was prayed for. The next meeting, she got up and testified that she had been wonderfully healed. She said, "I will be so happy to go and tell Mother about my healing."

She went to her home and testified to her wonderful healing. The next year when we were having the convention, she came again. From a human perspective, it looked as though the goiter was just as big as ever, but that young woman was believing God. Soon she was on her feet giving her testimony, saying, "I was here last year, and the Lord wonderfully healed me. I want to tell you that this has been the best year of my life." She seemed to be greatly blessed in that meeting, and she went home to testify more strongly than ever that the Lord had healed her.

She believed God. The third year, she was at the meeting again, and some people who looked at her said, "How big that goiter has become!" But when the time came for testimonies, she was on her feet and testified, "Two years ago, the Lord gloriously healed me of a goiter. I had a most wonderful healing. It is grand to be healed by the power of God."

That day, someone questioned her and said, "People will think there is something the matter with you. Why don't you look in the mirror? You will see that your goiter is bigger than ever."

The young woman went to the Lord about it and said, "Lord, You so wonderfully healed me two years ago. Won't You show all the people that You healed me?" She went to sleep peacefully that night still believing God. When she came down the next day, there was not a trace or a mark of that goiter.

A faint heart can never have a gift. Two things are essential: first, love; second, determination—a boldness of faith that will cause God to fulfill His Word—"according to the eternal purpose which [God] accomplished in Christ Jesus our Lord, in whom we have boldness and access with confidence through faith in Him" (Ephesians 3:11-12).

Thought for today: God wants to bring us into divine purity of heart and life, a holy boldness.

GOD NEVER FAILS

As it is written, "I have made you a father of many nations."
—Romans 4:17

Scripture reading: Genesis 15:3–6; 18:9–15

Here are Sarah—her body is almost dead—and Abraham—his body is almost dead. "Now," says Abraham, "God has made me a father of many nations, and there is no hope of a son according to the natural law, no hope whatever." Here God says, *"I have made you a father of many nations,"* yet Abraham has no son. During the past twenty years of waiting, conditions had grown more and more hopeless, yet the promise had been made.

How long have you believed and still suffered from some disease? How long have you been waiting for the promise, and it has not come? Look here! I want to tell you that all the people who are saved are blessed with faithful Abraham (Galatians 3:9). Abraham is the great substance of the whole keynote of Scripture. He is a man who dared for twenty-five years to believe God when everything got worse every day. If we will believe God, He will make us so different. This is a blessed incarnation of living faith that changes us and makes us know that "[God] *is, and that He is a rewarder of those who diligently seek Him"* (Hebrews 11:6). God is a reality. God is true, and in Him there is no lie or *"shadow of turning"* (James 1:17). Oh, it is good! I do love to think about such truths as these.

No subject in the whole Bible makes my body aflame with passion after God and His righteousness as this one about Abraham does. I see that God never fails. He wants man to believe, and then man will never fail. Oh, the loveliness of the character of God!

"A father of many nations." You talk about your infirmities—look at this! I have never felt I have had an infirmity since I understood this chapter. My cup runs over as I see the magnitude of this living God.

It is almost as if Abraham had said, "I won't look at my body. I won't look at my infirmities. I believe God will make the whole thing right." Some of us can say, "What does it matter if I have not heard for over twenty years? I believe my ears will be perfect." God is reality and wants us to know that if we will believe, it will be perfect. *"God…gives life to the dead and calls those things which do not exist as though they did"* (Romans 4:17).

I wonder if you really believe that God can quicken what is dead. I have seen it many times. The more there was no hope, Abraham believed in hope. Sometimes Satan will cloud your mind and interfere with your perception so that the obscure condition is brought right in between you and God, but God is able to change the whole position if you will let Him have a chance. Turn your back on every sense of unbelief and believe God. There are some who would like to feel the presence of the touch of God; God will bring it to you. I pray that you will come to this place.

Thought for today: God knows. He has a plan; He has a way. Do you dare trust Him?

FAITH NOT FEELINGS

*And not being weak in faith, he did not consider his own body,
already dead (since he was about a hundred years old), and the
deadness of Sarah's womb. He did not waver at the promise of God
through unbelief, but was strengthened in faith, giving glory to God.*
—Romans 4:19–20

Scripture reading: Romans 4:8–5:2

Sometimes I see that the power of God within us is greater when we are weak than when we are strong. We see this with Abraham in Genesis. The power in Abraham grew stronger as his body grew weaker. Looking at him, Sarah would shake her head and say, "I never saw anybody so thin and weak and helpless in my life. No, Abraham, I have been looking at you, and you seem to be going right down." But Abraham refused to look at his own body or Sarah's; he believed that the promise would happen.

Suppose you come for healing. You know as well as possible that, according to natural life, there is no virtue in your body to give you that health. You also know that the ailment from which you suffer has drained your life and energy so that there is no help in you at all, but God says you will be healed if you believe. It makes no difference how your body is. It was exactly the helplessness of Sarah and Abraham that brought the glorious fact that a son was born, and I want you to see what sort of a son he was.

He was the son of Abraham. His seed is the seed of the whole believing church—innumerable as the sands on the seashore. God wants us to know that there is no limitation with Him, and He wants to bring us to a place where there will be no limitation in us. This state can only be brought about by the working of the Omnipotent in the human body, working in us continually—the One who is greater than any science or any power in the world—and bringing us into the place to comprehend God and man.

Come now into a position of faith. I want you to see that you can be healed if you will just hear and believe the Word. Some people want healing; some want salvation; others want sanctification and the baptism of the Spirit. Romans 5:2 says it is by faith that we have access to grace. Grace is omnipotence; it is activity, benevolence, and mercy. It is truth, perfection, and God's inheritance in the soul that can believe. Grace is God. You open the door by faith, and God comes in with all you need and want. It cannot be otherwise, for it is *"of faith that it might be according to grace"* (Romans 4:16).

This is believing. Unfortunately, most people want healing *by feeling*. It cannot be. Some even want salvation on the same lines, and they say, "Oh, if only I could feel I was saved!" It will never come that way. God draws you to hear and believe the Scriptures, which can make you *"wise unto salvation"* (2 Timothy 3:15). The Scriptures open your understanding to the truth, so that you can open the door of faith and receive the answer to your requests.

Thought for today: Three things work together. The first is faith. Faith can always bring the second thing, fact, and fact can always bring the third thing, joy.

ALL THINGS ARE POSSIBLE

Jesus said to him, "If you can believe,
all things are possible to him who believes."
—Mark 9:23

Scripture reading: Mark 9:1–29

We have a wonderful God, a God whose ways are *"past finding out"* (Romans 11:33) and whose grace and power are limitless.

I was in Belfast one day and saw one of the brothers of the assembly. He said to me, "Wigglesworth, I am troubled. I have had a good deal of sorrow during the past five months. I had a woman in my church who could always pray the blessing of heaven down on our meetings. She is an old woman, but her presence is always an inspiration. Five months ago, she fell and broke her leg. The doctors put it into a cast, but when they removed the cast, the bones were not properly set, and she fell and broke the leg again."

He took me to her house, and there was a woman lying in a bed. I asked her, "Well, what about it now?"

She said, "They have sent me home incurable. The doctors say that I am so old that my bones won't knit. There is no strength in my bones. They could not do anything for me, and they say I will have to lie in bed for the rest of my life."

I said to her, "Can you believe God?"

She replied, "Yes, ever since I heard that you had come to Belfast, my faith has been quickened. If you will pray, I will believe. I know there is no power on earth that can make the bones of my leg knit, but I know that nothing is impossible with God."

I said, "Do you believe He will meet you now?"

She answered, "I do."

It is grand to see people believe God. God knew all about this leg and that it was broken in two places. I said to the woman, "When I pray, something will happen."

Her husband was sitting there; he had been in his chair for four years and could not walk a step. He called out, "I don't believe. I won't believe. You will never get me to believe."

I said, "All right," and laid my hands on his wife in the name of the Lord Jesus.

The moment hands were laid upon her, she cried out, "I'm healed."

I said, "I'm not going to assist you to rise. God will do it all." She arose and walked up and down the room, praising God.

The old man was amazed at what had happened to his wife, and he cried out, "Make me walk, make me walk."

I said to him, "You old sinner, repent." He cried out, "Lord, You know I believe."

I'm not sure he meant what he said at first; but the Lord was full of compassion. If He marked our sins, where would any of us be? God will always meet us if we believe all things are possible.

I laid my hands on him, and the power went right through the old man's body. For the first time in four years, those legs received power to carry his body. He walked up and down and in and out of the room. He said, "Oh, what great things God has done for us tonight!"

Thought for today: Desire God, and you will have desires from God.

THE WAY TO OVERCOME

Who is he who overcomes the world,
but he who believes that Jesus is the Son of God?
—1 John 5:5

Scripture reading: Revelation 3:1–12

The greatest weakness in the world is unbelief. The greatest power is the faith that works by love. Love, mercy, and grace are bound eternally to faith. Fear is the opposite of faith, but *"there is no fear in love"* (1 John 4:18). Those whose hearts are filled with a divine faith and love have no question in their hearts as to being caught up when Jesus comes.

The world is filled with fear, torment, remorse, and brokenness, but faith and love are sure to overcome. God has established the earth and humanity on the lines of faith. As you come into line, fear is cast out, the Word of God comes into operation, and you find bedrock. All the promises are *"Yes"* and *"Amen"* to those who believe (2 Corinthians 1:20).

When you have faith in Christ, the love of God is so real that you feel you could do anything for Jesus. Whoever believes, loves. *"We love Him because He first loved us"* (1 John 4:19). When did He love us? When we were in the mire. What did He say? *"Your sins are forgiven you"* (Luke 5:20). Why did He say it? Because He loved us. What for? That He might bring many sons into glory (Hebrews 2:10). What was His purpose? That we might be with Him forever.

The whole pathway is an education for this high vocation and calling. How glorious this hidden mystery of love is! For our sins there is the double blessing. *"Whatever is born of God overcomes the world. And this is the victory…our faith"* (1 John 5:4). To believe is to overcome.

I am heir to all the promises because I believe. It is a great heritage. I overcome because I believe the truth, and the truth makes me free (John 8:32). Christ is the root and source of our faith, and because He is in our faith, what we believe for will come to pass. There is no wavering. This is the principle: he who believes is definite. A definite faith brings a definite experience and a definite utterance.

There is no limit to the power God will cause to come upon those who cry to Him in faith, for God is rich to all who will call upon Him. Stake your claim for your children, your families, and your coworkers, so that many sons may be brought to glory. As your prayer rests upon the simple principle of faith, nothing will be impossible for you.

The root principle of all this divine overcoming faith in the human heart is Jesus Christ, and when you are grafted deeply into Him, you may win millions of lives to the faith. Jesus is *"the way, the truth, and the life"* (John 14:6). He is the answer to every hard problem in your heart.

Thought for today: As the day of the Lord hastens on, we too need to walk by faith until we overcome all things. By our simple belief in Jesus Christ, we walk right into glory.

WHAT ARE YOU FOCUSED ON?

And the prayer of faith will save the sick,
and the Lord will raise him up.
—James 5:15

Scripture reading: James 5:13–20

ABaptist minister came to me and said, "The doctor says that this is the last day that my wife has to live." I said, "Oh, Brother Clark, why don't you believe God? God can raise her up if you will only believe Him." He replied, "I have looked at you when you talked and have wept and said, 'Father, if You could give me this confidence, I would be so happy.'" I said, "Could you trust God?" I felt that the Lord would heal her.

I sent word to a man I knew and asked him to go with me. When he was on his knees, this man could pray by the hour. I told him that whatever his impression was to be sure to go on and pray right through. We entered the house, and I asked my friend to pray first. He began to cry in his desperation and prayed that this husband might be comforted after he was left with these little motherless children, and that he might be strengthened to bear his sorrow. I could hardly wait until he was finished; my whole being was shaking. I thought, "What an awful thing to bring this man all this way to pray that kind of a prayer of unbelief!" What was the matter with him? He was looking at the dying woman instead of looking at God. The Lord wants to help us right now to learn this truth and to keep our eyes on Him.

When this man had finished, I said to her husband, "Brother Clark, now you pray." He took up the thread where the other man had left off and went on with the same kind of prayer. He got so down beneath the burden that I thought he would never rise again, and I was glad when he was through. I could not have borne it much longer!

The prayers of these two men were the most out-of-place prayers that I had ever heard; the whole atmosphere was being charged with unbelief. My soul was stirred. I was eager for God to get a chance to have His way. I did not wait to pray but rushed up to the bed and tipped the oil bottle, pouring nearly the whole contents on the woman. Then I saw Jesus just above the bed with the sweetest smile on His face, and I said to her, "Woman, Jesus Christ makes you whole." The woman stood up, perfectly healed, and she is a strong woman today.

Oh, beloved, may God help us to get our eyes off the conditions and symptoms, no matter how bad they may be, and get them fastened on Him. Then we will be able to pray *"the prayer of faith."*

Thought for today: You can never pray *"the prayer of faith"* if you look at the person who is needing it; there is only one place to look and that is to Jesus.

DARE TO BELIEVE GOD

[Whoever] does not doubt in his heart, but believes that those things
he says will be done, he will have whatever he says.
Therefore I say to you, whatever things you ask when you pray,
believe that you receive them, and you will have them.
—Mark 11:23–24

Scripture reading: Mark 11

"He who believes." What a word! God's Word changes us, and we enter into fellowship and communion with Him. We enter into assurance and Godlikeness, for we see the truth and believe. Faith is an effective power; God opens the understanding and reveals Himself. *"Therefore it is of faith that it might be according to grace"* (Romans 4:16). Grace is God's blessing coming down to you. You open the door to God as an act of faith, and God does all you want.

Jesus drew the hearts of the people to Himself. They came to Him with all of their needs, and He relieved them all. He talked to men, healed the sick, relieved the oppressed, and cast out demons. *"He who believes in Me, the works that I do he will do also"* (John 14:12).

"He who believes in Me"—the essence of divine life is in us by faith. To the one who believes, it will come to pass. We become supernatural by the power of God. If you believe, the power of the enemy cannot stand, for God's Word is against him. Jesus gives us His Word to make faith effective. If you can believe in your heart, you begin to speak whatever you desire, and whatever you dare to say is done. You will have whatever you say after you believe in your heart (Mark 11:23–24). Dare to believe, and then dare to speak, for you will have whatever you say if you do not doubt.

Some time ago in England, the power of God was on the meeting, and I was telling the people they could be healed. I said that if they would rise up, I would pray for them, and the Lord would heal them. A man with broken ribs was healed. Then a fourteen-year-old girl said, "Will you pray for me?" After I prayed for her, she said, "Mother, I am being healed." She had straps on her feet, and when these were removed, God healed her right away.

A boy came into a meeting on crutches. He had a broken ankle. Several of us joined in prayer, and with joy I saw the boy so healed that he walked away carrying those crutches. Beloved, Jesus is coming soon. There are so many things that seem to say, "He is at the door." Will you use the power of Christ within you for His glory?

Thought for today: Dare to believe God, and it will be as you believe.

REMEMBER GOD'S GOODNESS

In all your ways acknowledge Him, and He shall direct your paths.
—Proverbs 3:6

Scripture reading: Proverbs 3:1–26

After Jesus had departed from the Pharisees, He said to His disciples, *"Take heed and beware of the leaven of the Pharisees and the Sadducees"* (Matthew 16:6). The disciples began to discuss this warning among themselves, and all they could think of was that they had brought no bread. What were they going to do? Then Jesus uttered these words: *"O you of little faith"* (v. 8). He had been with them for quite a while, yet they were still a great disappointment to Him because of their lack of comprehension and lack of faith. They could not grasp the profound spiritual truth He was bringing to them and could only think about having brought no bread. So Jesus said to them:

> *O you of little faith...Do you not yet understand, or remember the five loaves of the five thousand and how many baskets you took up? Nor the seven loaves of the four thousand and how many large baskets you took up?* (Matthew 16:8–10)

Do you keep in mind how God has been gracious in the past? God has done wonderful things for all of us. If we keep these things in mind, we will be *"strengthened in [our] faith"* (Romans 4:20). We should be able to defy Satan in everything. Remember that the Lord has led all the way. When Joshua passed over the Jordan on dry land, he told the people to pick up twelve stones and set them up in Gilgal. These were to be a constant reminder to the children of Israel that they came over the Jordan on dry land (Joshua 4:20–24). How many times had Jesus shown His disciples the mightiness of His power? Yet they failed in faith.

Our precious Lord Jesus has everything for everybody. Forgiveness of sins, healing of diseases, and the fullness of the Spirit all come from one source—the Lord Jesus Christ. Hear Him who is *"the same yesterday, today, and forever"* (Hebrews 13:8) as He announces the purpose for which He came:

> *The Spirit of the Lord is upon Me, because He has anointed Me to preach the gospel to the poor; He has sent Me to heal the brokenhearted, to proclaim liberty to the captives and recovery of sight to the blind, to set at liberty those who are oppressed; to proclaim the acceptable year of the Lord.*　　　　　　　　　　　　　　　(Luke 4:18–19)

Thought for today: The difference between those who are being led by the Holy Spirit and those who are being deceived by Satan is joy, gladness, and a calm expression instead of sadness, sorrow, and depression.

THE FULLNESS OF HIS WORD

Faith is the substance of things hoped for,
the evidence of things not seen.
—Hebrews 11:1

Scripture reading: Hebrews 11:1–10

We may be in a very low ebb of the tide, but it is good to be in a place where the tide can rise. Everything depends on our being filled with the Holy Spirit. If He can only get us in readiness for His plan to be worked out, it will be wonderful.

Everything depends on our believing God. If we are saved, it is only because God's Word says so. We cannot rest upon our feelings. We cannot do anything without a living faith. It is surely God Himself who comes to us in the person of His beloved Son and strengthens us so that we realize that our bodies are surrounded by His power. All things are possible for us in God.

God purposes that we might be on the earth to manifest His glory, that every time satanic power is confronted, God desires to be able to say of us as He did of Job, *"Have you considered My servant Job...a blameless and upright man?"* (Job 1:8). The joy of the Lord can be so clearly evidenced in us that we will be filled with God and able to rebuke the devil.

God has shown me in the night watches that everything that is not of faith is sin (Romans 14:23). God wants to bring us into harmony with His will so that we will see that if we do not believe all of the Word of God, something in us is not purely sanctified to accept the fullness of His Word. Many people put their human wisdom in the place of God, and God is not able to give the best to the person who is confronting God in such a way. God is not able to get the best through us until the human will is dissolved.

People say, "I want things to be tangible. I want something to appeal to my human reasoning." My response is that everything that you cannot see is eternal. Everything you see now will fade away and will be consumed, but what you cannot see, what is more real than you, is the substance of all things. God in the human soul is mightier than you by a million times.

We can never forget the fullness of God's Word: *"Faith is the substance of things hoped for, the evidence of things not seen"* (Hebrews 11:1).

Thought for today: There is nothing we can come short of if the Holy Spirit is the prime mover in our thoughts and lives, for He has a plan greater than ours.

GOD IS FOR YOU

If God is for us, who can be against us?
—Romans 8:31

Scripture reading: 1 John 4:16–5:5

It does not matter where you are if God is with you. He who is for you is a million times greater than all who can be against you. Oh, if by the grace of God we could only see that the blessings of God's divine power come to us with such sweetness, whispering to us, "Be still, My child. All is well." Be still and see the salvation of the Lord.

What would happen if we learned the secret to asking once and then believing? What an advantage it would be if we could come to a place where we know that everything is within reach of us. God wants us to see that every obstacle can be removed. God brings us into a place where the difficulties are, where the pressure is, where the hard corner is, where everything is so difficult that you know there are no possibilities on the human side. God must do it. All these places are in God's plan. God allows trials, difficulties, temptations, and perplexities to come along our path, but there is not a temptation or trial that can come to us without God providing a way out (1 Corinthians 10:13). You do not have the way out; it is God who can bring you through.

Many believers come to me and want me to pray for their nervous systems. I guarantee there is not a person in the whole world who could be nervous if he or she understood 1 John 4. Believe that God loves you!

And we have known and believed the love that God has for us. God is love, and he who abides in love abides in God, and God in him. Love has been perfected among us in this: that we may have boldness in the day of judgment; because as He is, so are we in this world. There is no fear in love; but perfect love casts out fear, because fear involves torment. But he who fears has not been made perfect in love. We love Him because He first loved us. (1 John 4:16–19)

God is separating us for Himself because of His love for us. If only all the saints knew how precious they are in the sight of God (Isaiah 43:4), they would scarcely be able to sleep when thinking of His watchful, loving care. Every expression of love is in the heart. When you begin to pour out your heart to God in love, your very being, your whole self, desires Him. Perfect love cannot fear (1 John 4:18).

Thought for today: Perfect love means that Jesus has taken hold of your intentions, desires, and thoughts and has purified everything.

HEARING BY THE WORD

Faith comes by hearing, and hearing by the word of God."
—Romans 10:17

Scripture reading: Romans 10

Do you not see that the words of the Master are the instructions of faith?

It is impossible for anything that Jesus says to miss. All His words are spirit and life. Jesus told us, *"The words that I speak to you are spirit, and they are life"* (John 6:63). If you will only have faith in Him, you will find that every word that God gives is life. You cannot be in close contact with Him and receive His Word in simple faith without feeling the effect of it in your body, as well as in your spirit and soul.

A woman came to me in Cardiff, Wales, who was filled with ulcers. She had fallen in the streets twice because of this trouble. When she came to the meeting, it seemed as if the evil power within her purposed to kill her right there. She fell, and the power of the devil was attacking her severely. Not only was she helpless, but it seemed as if she had died.

I cried, "O God, help this woman." Then I rebuked the evil power in the name of Jesus, and instantly the Lord healed her. She rose up and made a great to-do. She felt the power of God in her body and wanted to testify continually. After three days, she went to another place and began to testify about the Lord's power to heal.

She came to me and said, "I want to tell everyone about the Lord's healing power. Don't you have any tracts on this subject?" I handed her my Bible and said, "Matthew, Mark, Luke, and John—they are the best tracts on healing. They are full of incidents of the healing power of Jesus. They will never fail to accomplish the work of God if people will only read and believe them."

That is where men are lacking. All lack of faith is due to not feeding on God's Word. You need it every day. How can you enter into a life of faith? Feed on the living Christ of whom this Word is full. As you are taken up with the glorious fact and the wondrous presence of the living Christ, the faith of God will spring up within you. *"Faith comes by hearing, and hearing by the word of God"* (Romans 10:17).

God desires to build us up in this faith so that we are living in great expectation. He is bringing us into a place with Himself where we can say, "I have seen God."

Thought for today: We must be firmer in our faith today than we were yesterday.

MORE PRECIOUS THAN GOLD

*That the genuineness of your faith, being much more precious than
gold that perishes, though it is tested by fire, may be found to praise,
honor, and glory at the revelation of Jesus Christ.*
—1 Peter 1:7

Scripture reading: 1 Peter 1

Some of you wonder what is up when you are not healed in a moment.
God never breaks His promise. The trial of your faith is *"much more precious than gold."*

God wants to destroy the power of the devil. He wants to move you
so that in the face of hardships, you will praise the Lord. *"Count it all joy"*
(James 1:2). You have to take a leap today; you have to leap into the promises. You have to believe that God never fails you; you have to believe it is
impossible for God to break His word. He is *"from everlasting to everlasting"* (Psalm 90:2).

Forever and ever, not for a day,
He keepeth His promise forever;
To all who believe,
To all who obey,
He keepeth His promise forever.

There is no variableness with God, no *"shadow of turning"* (James 1:17).
He is the same. He manifests His divine glory.

Jesus said to Mary and Martha, *"If you would believe you would see the
glory of God"* (John 11:40). We must understand that there will be times
of testing, but they are only to make us more like the Master. He was *"in*

all points tempted as we are, yet without sin" (Hebrews 4:15). He endured all things. He is our example.

Oh, that God would place us in an earnest, intent position in which flesh and blood have to yield to the Spirit of God! We will go forward; we will not be moved by our feelings.

Suppose that a man who is prayed for today receives a blessing, but tomorrow he begins murmuring because he does not feel exactly as he wants to feel. What is he doing? He is replacing the Word of God with his feelings. What a disgrace! Let God have His perfect work. The price for all was paid by the blood of Jesus Christ at Calvary. Oh, He is the living God, the One who has power to change us! *"It is He who has made us, and not we ourselves"* (Psalm 100:3). And it is He who purposes to transform us so that the greatness of His power may work through us.

We have a big God. We have a wonderful Jesus. We have a glorious Comforter. God's canopy is over you and will cover you at all times, preserving you from evil. *"Under His wings you shall take refuge"* (Psalm 91:4).

The Word of God is *"living and powerful"* (Hebrews 4:12), and in its treasures you will find eternal life. If you dare trust this wonderful Lord, this Lord of Life, you will find in Him everything you need. Oh, beloved, God delights in us, and when a man's ways please the Lord, then He makes all things move according to His own blessed purpose.

Thought for today: God has you on this earth for the purpose of bringing out His character in you.

BY FAITH

By grace you have been saved through faith,
and that not of yourselves; it is the gift of God.
—Ephesians 2:8

Scripture reading: Hebrews 11

By *faith Abel offered to God a more excellent sacrifice than Cain"* (Hebrews 11:4); *"by faith Enoch was taken away so that he did not see death"* (v. 5); *"by faith Noah…prepared an ark for the saving of his household"* (v. 7); *"by faith Abraham obeyed when he was called to go out to the place which he would receive as an inheritance"* (v. 8).

There is only one way to all the treasures of God, and that is the way of faith. All things are possible, even the fulfilling of all promises is possible, to him who believes (Mark 9:23).

There will be failure in our lives if we do not build on the base, the Rock, Christ Jesus. He is the only way; He is the truth; He is the life (John 14:6). And the Word He gives us is life-giving. As we receive the Word of Life, it quickens, it opens, it fills us, it moves us, it changes us, and it brings us into a place where we dare to say amen to all that God has said.

Beloved, there is a lot in an amen. You never get any place until you have the amen inside of you. That was the difference between Zacharias and Mary. When the Word came to Zacharias, he was filled with unbelief until the angel said, *"You will be mute…because you did not believe my words"* (Luke 1:20). Mary said, *"Let it be to me according to your word"* (v. 38). The Lord was pleased that she believed what He had spoken. When we believe what God has said, there will be results.

We may do much praying and groaning, but we do not receive from God because of that; we receive because we believe. Yet sometimes it takes

God a long time to bring us through the groaning and the crying before we can believe.

I know that no man by his praying can change God, for you cannot change Him. Charles Finney said, "Can a man who is full of sin and all kinds of ruin in his life change God when he starts to pray?" No, it is impossible. But when a man labors in prayer, he groans and travails because his tremendous sin is weighing him down, and he becomes broken in the presence of God. When properly melted, he comes into perfect harmony with the divine plan of God, and then God can work in that clay. He could not before. Prayer changes hearts, but it never changes God. He is *the same yesterday, today, and forever"* (Hebrews 13:8): full of love, full of compassion, full of mercy, full of grace, and ready to bestow this and communicate that to us as we come to Him in faith.

Believe that when you come into the presence of God, you can have all you came for. You can take it away and you can use it, for all the power of God is at your disposal in response to your faith.

Thought for today: All people are born with a natural faith, but God calls us to a supernatural faith that is a gift from Himself.

THE GIFT OF FAITH

*But one and the same Spirit works all these things, distributing to
each one individually as He wills.*
—1 Corinthians 12:11

Scripture reading: Ephesians 3

People ask me, "Do you have the gift of faith?" My response is that it is an important gift, but that what is still more important is for us to be making an advancement in God every moment.

Looking at the Word of God, I find that its realities are greater to me today than they were yesterday. It is the most sublime, joyful truth that God always brings an enlargement. Nothing dead, dry, or barren is in this life of the Spirit. God is always moving us on to something higher, and as we move on in the Spirit, our faith will always rise to each occasion. This is how the gift of faith is manifested. You see something, and you know that your own faith is nothing in the situation.

One day, I was in San Francisco sitting on a streetcar, and I saw a boy in great agony on the street. I said, "Let me get out." I rushed to where the boy was. He was in agony because of stomach cramps. I put my hand on his stomach in the name of Jesus. The boy jumped up and stared at me with astonishment. He found himself instantly free of pain. The gift of faith dared in the face of everything. It is as we are in the Spirit that the Spirit of God will operate this gift anywhere and at any time.

Once a woman rose in a meeting asking for prayer. I prayed for her, and she was healed. She cried out, "It is a miracle! It is a miracle! It is a miracle!" That is what God wants to do for us all the time as our faith arises to the occasion. As surely as we get free in the Holy Spirit, something will happen. Let us pursue the best things, and let God have His right-of-way.

When the Spirit of God is operating this gift within a person, He causes him to know what God is going to do. When the man with the withered hand was in the synagogue, Jesus got all the people to look to see what would happen. The gift of faith always knows the results. Jesus said to the man, *"Stretch out your hand"* (Matthew 12:13). His words had creative force. He was not living on the edge of speculation. He spoke and something happened. He is the Son of God, and He came to bring us into sonship. He was the *"firstfruits"* of the resurrection (1 Corinthians 15:20), and He calls us to be *"firstfruits"* (James 1:18), to be like Him.

Thought for today: God cannot trust some people with a gift, but He can trust those who have a humble, broken, contrite heart (Isaiah 66:2).

FULL OF FAITH AND POWER

Stephen, full of faith and power, did great wonders and signs.
—Acts 6:8

Scripture reading: Luke 4:1–19

In the early days of the church, all who did the work of serving had to be full of the Holy Spirit. The greatest qualification for ministry is to be filled with the Spirit.

Stephen was a man *"full of faith and the Holy Spirit"* (Acts 6:5). God so manifested Himself in Stephen's body that he became an epistle of truth, known and read by all. He was full of faith!

Such men never talk doubtfully. You never hear them say, "I wish it could be so," or "If it is God's will." They have no *ifs*; they know. You never hear them say, "Well, it is not always so." They say, "It is sure to be." They laugh at impossibilities and cry, "It will be done!" They shout while the walls are up and when they come down. God has this faith for us in Christ. We must be careful that no unbelief and no wavering are found in us.

"Stephen, full of faith and power, did great wonders and signs among the people" (Acts 6:8). The Holy Spirit could do mighty things through him because he believed God, and God is with the man who dares to believe His Word. All things were possible because of the Holy Spirit's position in Stephen's body. Because Stephen was full of the Holy Spirit, God could fulfill His purposes through him.

When a child of God is filled with the Holy Spirit, the Spirit *"makes intercession for the saints according to the will of God"* (Romans 8:27). He fills us with longings and desires until we are in a place of fervency like a glowing fire. When we do not know what to do, the Holy Spirit begins to work. When the Holy Spirit has liberty in the body, He conveys all prayers into the presence of God. Such prayers are always heard. Such praying is always answered; it is never bare of result. When we are praying in the Holy Spirit, faith is evident, and as a result the power of God can be manifested in our midst.

It is God's desire to make us a new creation, with all the old things passed away and all things within us truly of God, to bring in a new, divine order, a perfect love, and an unlimited faith (2 Corinthians 5:17).

It is God's desire to fill you with His Holy Spirit. Will you accept God's plan for you? Redemption is free. Arise in the activity of faith, and God will heal you as you rise. When we are filled with the Holy Spirit, we will have wisdom, and we will have power. May God bless His Word and fill us full of His Holy Spirit.

Thought for today: Through the power of the Holy Spirit, may He reveal Christ in us more and more.

THE POWER OF THE SPIRIT

And they were all filled with the Holy Spirit.
—Acts 2:4

Scripture reading: Acts 2:1–21

One night, I was entrusted with a meeting, and I was guarding my position before God. I wanted approval from the Lord. I understood that God wants men full of the Holy Spirit, with divine ability, filled with life, a flaming fire. In the meeting, a young man stood up. He was a pitiful object with a face full of sorrow. I asked, "What is it, young man?"

He said he was unable to work, and he could scarcely walk. He said, "I am so helpless. I have tuberculosis and a weak heart, and my body is full of pain."

I said, "I will pray for you." I said to the people, "As I pray for this young man, you look at his face and see it change."

As I prayed, his face changed. I said to him, "Go out, run a mile, and come back to the meeting."

He came back and said, "I can now breathe freely."

The meetings were continuing, and I missed him. After a few days, I saw him again in a meeting. I said, "Young man, tell the people what God has done for you."

"Oh," he said, "I have been able to work and make money."

Praise God, this wonderful stream of the Holy Spirit never runs dry. You can take a drink; it is close to you. It is a river that is running deep, and there is plenty for all.

In another meeting, a man rose and said, "Will you touch me? I am in a terrible situation. I have a large family, but because of an accident in the pit, I have had no work for two years. I cannot open my hands." As I moved to pray, something happened that had never happened before. I put out my hand and before my hands reached his, he was loosed and made perfectly free. We are in the infancy of this wonderful outpouring of the Holy Spirit, and there is so much more for us!

I see that Stephen, full of faith and of power, did great wonders and miracles among the people. This same Holy Spirit can fill you, too, and then wonderous things will be accomplished. God will grant it. God is ready to touch and transform you right now. May the Lord open our eyes to see Him and to know that He is deeply interested in all that concerns us. He is *"touched with the feeling of our infirmities"* (Hebrews 4:15 KJV).

All things are naked and open to the eyes of Him with whom we are connected (Hebrews 4:13). He knows about that asthma. He knows about that rheumatism. He knows about that pain in the back, head, or feet. He wants to loose every captive and to set you free just as He has set me free by the working of His Holy Spirit. I am free from every human ailment, absolutely free.

Christ has redeemed us. Will you have it? It is yours; it is a perfect redemption. The Spirit of God will always reveal the Lord Jesus Christ. Serve Him; love Him; be filled with Him. It is lovely to hear Him as He makes Himself known to us. He is *"the same yesterday, today, and forever"* (Hebrews 13:8).

Thought for today: God is willing to fill us with the Holy Spirit and faith just as He filled Stephen.

ENERGIZED BY THE SPIRIT

When they had prayed, the place where they were assembled together
was shaken; and they were all filled with the Holy Spirit, and they
spoke the word of God with boldness.
—Acts 4:31

Scripture reading: Ephesians 3:14–21

It is a necessity for every one of us to be filled with God. It is not sufficient to have just a touch or to be filled with just a desire. Only one thing will meet the needs of the people, and that is for you to be immersed in the life of God. This means that God takes you and fills you with His Holy Spirit until you live right in Him. He does this so that *"whether you eat or drink, or whatever you do, [it may be] all to the glory of God"* (1 Corinthians 10:31). In that place you will find that all your strength and all your mind and all your soul are filled with a zeal, not only for worship, but also for proclamation. This proclamation is accompanied by all the power of God, which must move satanic power and disturb the world.

The reason the world is not seeing Jesus is that Christian people are not filled with Jesus. They are not filled with the Holy Spirit. They are satisfied with attending meetings weekly, reading the Bible occasionally, and praying sometimes.

Beloved, if God lays hold of you by the Holy Spirit, you will find that there is an end of everything and a beginning in God. Your whole body will become seasoned with a divine likeness of God. He will not only begin to use you, but also take you in hand, so that you might be *"a vessel for honor"* (2 Timothy 2:21).

Our lives are not to be lived for ourselves, for if we live for ourselves, we will die (Romans 8:13), but if *"by the Spirit [we] put to death the deeds of the* body, [we] *will live*" (v. 13). He who lives in the Spirit is subject to the powers of God, but he who lives for himself will die. The man who lives in the Holy Spirit lives a life of freedom, joy, blessing, and service—a life that brings blessing to others. God wants us to see that we must live in the Holy Spirit.

Beloved, the Holy Spirit is the Comforter. The Holy Spirit did not come to speak of Himself, but He came to unveil Him who said, *"Take My yoke upon you and learn from Me, for I am gentle and lowly in heart, and you will find rest for your souls"* (Matthew 11:29).

The Holy Spirit came to fill you with resurrection power, and He came so that you would be anointed with fresh oil that overflows in the splendor of His almightiness. Then right through you will come forth a river of divine anointing that will sustain you in the bitterest place. It will give life to the deadest formality, and say to the weak, *"Be strong"* (Deuteronomy 31:6). *"He gives power to the weak, and to those who have no might He increases strength"* (Isaiah 40:29). Possibility is the greatest thing of your life.

Thought for today: Jesus came to bring back to us what was forfeited in the garden.

AFLAME FOR GOD

[He] makes His angels spirits and His ministers a flame of fire.
—Hebrews 1:7

Scripture reading: Hebrews 1

God's ministers are to be flames of fire! It seems to me that no man with a vision, especially a vision by the Holy Spirit's power, can read that wonderful verse without being kindled to such a flame of fire for his Lord that it seems as if it would burn up everything that would interfere with his progress.

A flame of fire! It is a perpetual fire, a constant fire, a continual burning, a holy, inward flame, which is exactly what God's Son was in the world. God has nothing less for us than to be flames! It seems to me that if Pentecost, the baptism of the Holy Spirit, is to rise and be effective, we must have a living faith so that Christ's great might and power can flow through us until our lives become energized, moved, and aflame for God. The important point here is that the Holy Spirit has come to make Jesus King.

An opportunity to be a flame of fire for God came when I was traveling from Egypt to Italy. What I now tell you truly happened. On the ship and everywhere, God had been with me. A man on the ship suddenly collapsed; his wife was in a terrible state, and everybody else seemed to be too. Some said that he would die, but oh, to be a flame, to have the living Christ and His Holy Spirit dwelling within you!

We are backslidden if we have to pray for power, if we have to wait until we feel a sense of His presence. The baptism of the Holy Spirit has come upon you: *"You shall receive power when the Holy Spirit has come upon you"* (Acts 1:8). Within you is a greater power than there is in the world (1 John

4:4). Oh, to be awakened out of our unbelief into a place of daring for God on the authority of the blessed Book!

So in the name of Jesus, I rebuked the devil, and to the astonishment of the man's wife and the man himself, he was able to stand. He said, "What is this? It is going all over me. I have never felt anything like this before." From the top of his head to the soles of his feet, the power of God shook him. God has given us authority over the power of the devil. Oh, that we may live in the place where His glory excels! It would make anyone a flame of fire.

Thought for today: When we are baptized in the Holy Spirit, it is to crown Jesus King in our lives.

THE FIRE OF THE SPIRIT

John answered, saying to all, "I indeed baptize you with water; but One mightier than I is coming, whose sandal strap I am not worthy to loose. He will baptize you with the Holy Spirit and fire.
—Luke 3:16

Scripture reading: Luke 3:1–15

The baptism of the Holy Spirit has come for nothing less than to possess the whole of our lives. It sets up Jesus as King, and nothing can stand in His holy presence when He is made King. Everything will wither before Him. The inheritance of the Holy Spirit is given to every man *"for the profit of all"* (1 Corinthians 12:7). Praise the Lord! In the presence of the Holy Spirit, we have to *"come short in no gift"* (1 Corinthians 1:7).

This same Jesus has come for one purpose: that He might be made so manifest in us that the world will see Him. We must be burning and shining lights to reflect such a holy Jesus. We cannot do it with cold, indifferent experiences, and we never will. His servants are to be flames. Jesus is the life, and the Holy Spirit is the breath. He breathes through us the life of the Son of God, and we give it to others, and it gives life everywhere.

You should have been with me in Ceylon! I was having meetings in a Wesleyan chapel. The leaders there said, "What are we going to do? We are not touching the people here at all."

I said, "Can you have a meeting early in the morning, at eight o'clock? We will tell all the mothers who want their babies to be healed and all the old people over seventy to come. After that, I hope to give an address to all the people to make them ready for the Holy Spirit."

Oh, it would have done you all good to see four hundred mothers there with their babies! And then to see one hundred and fifty older people, with their white hair, coming to be healed. I believe that you need to have something more than smoke to touch people; you need to be a burning light. His ministers must be flames of fire.

Thousands gathered outside the chapel to hear the Word of God. There were about three thousand people crying for mercy at the same time. It was a glorious sight. After that, attendance at the meetings rose every night, five to six thousand people gathered there for preaching and prayer in a temperature of 110 degrees. I tell you, a flame of fire can do anything. Things change in the fire. This is Pentecost!

What moved me more than anything else was this—and I say this carefully and humbly because I would not like to mislead anybody—there were hundreds who tried to touch me because they were so impressed with the power of God in that place. And they testified everywhere that with a touch, they were healed. It was *not* the power of Wigglesworth. It was because they had the same faith that was with those at Jerusalem who believed that Peter's shadow would heal them (Acts 5:14–15).

What do you want? Is anything too hard for God? God can meet you now. God sees inwardly. He knows all about you. Nothing is hidden from Him, and He can satisfy the soul and give you a spring of eternal blessing that will carry you right through.

Thought for today: You can receive something in three minutes that you can carry with you into glory.

FILLED WITH THE SPIRIT

*Be filled with the Spirit, speaking to one another in psalms
and hymns and spiritual songs, singing and making
melody in your heart to the Lord.*
—Ephesians 5:18–19

Scripture reading: Ephesians 5:15–21

God wants to make us pillars: honorable, strong, and holy. God will move us on by His Holy Spirit. I am enamored with the possibility of this. God wants you to know that you are saved, cleansed, delivered, and marching to victory. He has given you the faith to believe. God has a plan for you! *"Set your mind on things above"* (Colossians 3:2) and get into the heavenly places with Christ.

"When Christ who is our life appears" (Colossians 3:4). Can I have any life apart from Him, any joy or any fellowship apart from Him? Jesus said, *"The ruler of this world is coming, and he has nothing in Me"* (John 14:30). All that is contrary in us is withered by the indwelling life of the Son of God.

Are we ready for all that God has for us? Have we been clothed with the Holy Spirit? Has mortality been swallowed up in life? If He who is our life came, we should go. I know that the Lord laid His hand on me. He filled me with the Holy Spirit.

Heaven has begun within me. I am happy and free now, since the Comforter has come. The Comforter is the great Revealer of the kingdom of God. He came to give us the more abundant life. God has designed the plan, and nothing else really matters because the Lord loves us. God sets great store in us.

The way into glory is through the flesh being torn away from the world and separated unto God. This freedom of spirit, freedom from the law of sin and death, is cause for rejoicing every day. The perfect law destroys the natural law. Spiritual activity takes in every passing ray, ushering in the days of heaven upon earth, when there is no sickness and when we do not even remember that we have bodies. The life of God changes us and brings us into the heavenly realm, where our reign over principalities and over all evil is limitless, powerful, and supernatural.

If the natural body decays, the Spirit renews. Spiritual power increases until, with one mind and one heart, the glory is brought down over all the earth, right on into divine life. When the whole life is filled, this is Pentecost come again. The life of the Lord will be manifested wherever we are, whether in a bus, in a car, or on a train. We will be filled with the life of Jesus unto perfection, rejoicing in hope of the glory of God (Romans 5:2), always looking for our translation into heaven.

I must have the overflowing life in the Holy Spirit. God is not pleased with anything less. It is a disgrace to be part of an ordinary plan after we are filled with the Holy Spirit. We are to be salt in the earth (Matthew 5:13). We are to be hot, not lukewarm (Revelations 3:16), which means seeing God with eagerness, liberty, movement, and power. Believe! Believe!

Thought for today: The life of the Lord in us draws us as a magnet, with His life filling up all else.

WHAT GOD CAN DO THROUGH YOU

And these signs will follow those who believe: In My name they will
cast out demons; they will speak with new tongues
—Mark 16:17

Scripture reading: Mark 16

You have no idea what God can do through you when you are filled with His Spirit. Every day and every hour, you can have the divine leading of God.

To be filled with the Holy Spirit is great in every respect. I have seen some who had been suffering for years, but when they have been filled with the Holy Spirit, every bit of their sickness has passed away. The Spirit of God has made real to them the life of Jesus, and they have been completely liberated from every sickness and infirmity.

At a meeting I was holding, the Lord was working, and many were being healed. A man saw what was taking place and remarked, "I'd like to try this thing." He came up for prayer and told me that his body was broken in two places. I laid my hands on him in the name of the Lord and said to him, "Now believe God."

The next night, he was at the meeting, and he got up like a lion. He shouted, "I want to tell you people that this man here is deceiving you. He laid his hands on me last night for a rupture in two places, but I'm not a bit better." I stopped him and said, "You are healed; your trouble is that you won't believe it."

He came back to the meeting the third night and when there was opportunity for testimonies, this man arose. He said, "I'm a mason by trade. Today I was working with a laborer, and he had to put a big stone in place. I helped him and did not feel any pain. I said to myself, 'How did I do that?' I went to a private place where I could take off my clothes, and I found that I was healed."

With joy, I told the people, "Last night, this man was against the Word of God, but now he believes it. It is true that *'these signs will follow those who believe…they will lay hands on the sick, and they will recover'* (Mark 16:17–18). Healing is through the power that is in the name of Jesus Christ." It is the Spirit who has come to reveal this by the Word of God and to make it spirit and life to us (John 6:63).

Thought for today: Some of you would like a touch in your bodies; some would like a touch in your spirit; some would like to be baptized in the Holy Spirit; some want to be filled with all God's power. It is there for you.

PRAYING IN THE SPIRIT

I will pray with the spirit,
and I will also pray with the understanding.
—1 Corinthians 14:15

Scripture reading: Hebrews 7:11–28

I am going to give you a very important word about the usefulness of praying in the Spirit. Lots of people are still without an understanding of what it is to pray in the Spirit. I am going to tell you a story that will help you to see how necessary it is that you be so lost in the presence of the Holy Spirit that you will pray in the Spirit.

Our missionary work in the center of Africa was opened by Brothers Burton and Salter, the latter being my daughter's husband. When they went there, there were four of them: Brothers Burton and Salter, an old man who wanted to help them build, and a young man who believed he was called to go. The old man died on the road and the young man turned back, so there were only two left.

They worked and labored. God was with them in a wonderful way. But Burton took sick, and all hopes were gone. Fevers are dreadful there; mosquitoes swarm; great evils are there. There he was, laid out in bed; there was no hope. They covered him and went outside very sorrowfully because he truly was a pioneer missionary. They were in great distress and uttered words like this, "He has preached his last sermon."

While they were in that state, without any prompting whatever, Brother Burton stood right in the midst of them. He had arisen from his bed and had walked outside, and he now stood beside them. They were astonished and asked how and what had happened! All he could say was that he had been awakened out of a deep sleep with a warm thrill that went over his head, right down his body, and out through his toes. "I feel so well," he said. "I don't know anything about my sickness."

It remained a mystery. Later, when he was in England visiting, a woman said to him, "Brother Burton, do you keep a diary?" "Yes," he answered. "Don't open the diary," she said, "until I talk with you." "All right," he said.

This is the story she told.

"At a certain time on a certain day, the Spirit of the Lord moved upon me. I was so moved by the power of the Spirit that I went alone into a place to pray. As I went there, believing that, just as usual, I was going to open my mouth and pray, the Spirit laid hold of me and I began praying in the Spirit—not with understanding, but in the Spirit.

"As I prayed, I saw right into Africa; I saw you laid out helpless and, to all appearances, apparently dead. I prayed on until the Spirit lifted me, I knew I was in victory, and I saw you had risen up from that bed.

"Look at your diary, will you?"

He looked in the diary and found that it was exactly the same day.

So there are revivals to come; there are wonderful things to be done, when we can be lost in the Spirit until the Spirit prays through to victory.

Thought for today: Prayer is without accomplishment unless it is accompanied by faith.

USED BY THE SPIRIT

But we have this treasure in earthen vessels, that the excellence of the
power may be of God and not of us.
—2 Corinthians 4:7

Scripture reading: 2 Corinthians 4

One day, in England, a lady wrote to ask if I would come and help her. She said she was blind, having two blood clots behind her eyes. I had been in London recently, and I didn't feel I wanted to go. However, I sent a letter, not knowing who she was, saying that if she was willing to go into a room with me and shut the door and never come out until she had perfect sight, I would come. She sent word, "Oh, come!"

The moment I reached the house, they brought in this blind woman. After we shook hands, she made her way to a room, opened the door, allowed me to go in, and then came in and shut the door. "Now," she said, "we are with God."

Have you ever been there? It is a lovely place.

In an hour and a half, the power of God fell upon us. Rushing to the window, she exclaimed, "I can see! Oh, I can see! The blood is gone; I can see!" Sitting down in a chair, she asked, "Could I receive the Holy Spirit?"

"Yes," I replied, "if all is right with God."

"You don't know me," she continued, "but for ten years I have been fighting your position. I couldn't bear these tongues, but God settled it today. I want the baptism of the Holy Spirit."

After she had prayed and repented of what she had said about tongues, she was filled with the Holy Spirit and began speaking in tongues.

When you put your hands upon people to pray, you can tell when the Holy Spirit is present. And if you will only yield to the Holy Spirit and allow Him to move, my word, what will happen!

See what the Word of God says, *"No one can say that Jesus is Lord except by the Holy Spirit"* (1 Corinthians 12:3). *"Lord!"* Bless God forever. Oh, for Him to be Lord and Master! For Him to rule and control! For Him to be filling your whole body with the plan of truth! Because you are in Christ Jesus, all things are subject to Him. It is lovely, and God wants to make it so to you. When you get there, you will find divine power continually working.

I absolutely believe that no person comes into the place of revelation and activity of the gifts of the Spirit except by this fulfilled promise of Jesus that He will baptize us in the Holy Spirit.

Thought for today: The Lord Jesus wants those who preach the Word to have the Holy Spirit in evidence in their lives.

WHAT IS YOUR GREATEST DESIRE?

I desire therefore that the men pray everywhere, lifting up holy hands,
without wrath and doubting.
—1 Timothy 2:8

Scripture reading: 1 Timothy 3

I remember when I was at Antwerp and Brussels. The power of God was very mighty upon me there. Going on to London, I called on some friends. To show you the leading of the Lord, these friends said, "Oh, the Holy Spirit sent you here. How much we need you!"

There was a young man twenty-six years old who had been in bed eighteen years. His body was much bigger than an ordinary body because of inactivity, but his legs were like a child's. He had never been able to dress himself. When his family received the wire saying we were coming, the father dressed the young man. He was sitting in a chair when we arrived. I felt it was one of the opportunities of my life.

"What is the greatest desire of your heart?" I asked this young man. "Oh," he said, "to be filled with the Holy Spirit!" I put my hands on him and said, "Receive; receive the Hoy Spirit." Instantly, he became drunk with the Spirit and fell off the chair like a big bag of potatoes. I saw what God could do with a paralyzed man. First, his head began shaking terrifically; then his back began moving very fast, and then his legs. Then he spoke clearly in tongues, and we wept and praised the Lord.

Looking at his legs, I saw that they were still as they had been, by all appearances, and this is where I missed it. These "missings" are sometimes God's opportunities of teaching us important lessons. He will teach us through our weaknesses what is not faith. It was not faith for me to look at that body, but human nature. The man who wants to work the works of God must never look at conditions but at Jesus, in whom everything is complete.

I looked at the boy, and there was absolutely no help in the natural. I turned to the Lord and said, "Lord, tell me what to do," and He did. He said, "Command him to walk in My name." This is where I missed it again. Instead, I got the father to help me lift him up to see if his legs had strength. We did our best, but he and I together could not move him. Then the Lord showed me my mistake, and I said, "God, forgive me." I got right down and repented and said to the Lord, "Please tell me again."

God is so good. He never leaves us to ourselves. Again, He said to me, "Command him in My name to walk." So I shouted, "Arise and walk in the name of Jesus!" Did he do it? No, I declare he never walked. He was lifted up by the power of God in a moment, and he *ran*. The door was wide open; he ran out across the road into a field where he ran up and down and came back. Oh, it was a miracle!

Thought for today: We have left the old order of things. If we go back, we miss God's plan.

MINISTERING THE GIFTS OF HEALINGS, PART 1

To another gifts of healings by the same Spirit.
—1 Corinthians 12:9

Scripture reading: Psalm 65

Now I will deal with the gift of healing itself. It is actually "gifts of healings," not the "gift" of healing. Gifts of healings can deal with every case of sickness, every disease that there is. These gifts are so full that they are beyond human expression, but you come into the fullness of them as the light brings revelation to you.

I have people continually coming to me and saying, "When you are preaching, I see a halo around you," or "When you are preaching, I have seen angels standing around you."

I hear these things from time to time, and I am thankful that people have such spiritual vision. I do not have that kind of vision; however, I have the express glory of the Lord covering me, the intense inner working of His power. As a result, often when I stand to teach, I do not have to choose the words to speak. The language has been chosen, the thoughts have been chosen, and I have been speaking in prophecy more than in any other way. In this way, I know we have been in the school of the Holy Spirit in a great way.

The only vision I have had in a divine healing meeting is this: often, when I have laid hands upon the people, I have seen two hands go before my hands. This has happened many, many times.

The person who has the gifts of healing does not look to see what is happening. After I finish ministering, many things are manifested, but they don't move me. I am not moved by anything I see. The divine gifts of healings are so profound in the person who has them that there is no such thing as doubt, and there could not be; whatever happens could not change the person's opinion or thought or act. He expects the very thing that God intends him to have as he lays hands upon the seeker.

Wherever I go, the manifestation of divine healing is considerably greater after I leave than when I am there. Why? It is God's plan for me. God has great grace over me. Wonderful things have been accomplished, and people have told me what happened when I was there, but these things were hidden from me. God has a reason why He hides things from me.

When I lay hands upon people for a specific thing, I tell you, that thing will take place. I believe it will be so, and I never turn my ears or my eyes from the fact. It has to be so. The gifts of healing are a fact. They are a production; they are a faith; they are an unwavering trust; they are a confidence; they are a reliability.

Thought for today: Here are three of the leading principles of the baptism in the Holy Spirit: it is ministry; it is operation; it is manifestation! We must see to it that God is producing these three through us.

MINISTERING THE GIFTS OF HEALINGS, PART 2

For to one is given...gifts of healings.
—1 Corinthians 12:8–9

Scripture reading: 1 Corinthians 12:4–11

The gifts of healings are wonderful gifts from the Holy Spirit. Remember, there is a difference between having a gift of healing and *"gifts of healings."* God doesn't want us to come short in anything (1 Corinthians 1:7). I like this term *"gifts of healings."* To have these gifts, I must bring myself into conformity with the mind and will of God.

How is it possible to minister the gifts of healings considering the peculiarities there are in various churches and the many evil powers of Satan that confront us and possess bodies?

Some people think by the way I went about praying for the sick that I was sometimes unloving and rough. But oh, friends, you have no idea what I see behind the sickness and the one who is afflicted. I am not dealing with the person; I am dealing with the satanic forces that are binding the afflicted. As far as people go, my heart is full of love and compassion for all, but I fail to see how you will ever reach a place where God will be able to use you until you get angry at the devil.

One day, a pet dog followed a lady out of her house and ran all around her feet. She said to the dog, "I cannot have you with me today." The dog wagged its tail and made a great fuss. "Go home, pet," she said kindly, but it didn't go. At last, she shouted roughly, "Go home!" and off it went.

Some people play with the devil like that. "Poor thing," they say. The devil can stand all the comfort anybody in the world wants to give him.

Cast him out! You are not dealing with the person; you are dealing with the devil. If you say with authority, "Come out, you demons, in the name of Jesus!" they must come out. You will always be right when you dare to treat sickness as the devil's work.

Gifts of healings are so varied that you will often find the gift of discernment operating in connection with them. Moreover, the manifestations of the Spirit are given to us "*for the profit of all*" (1 Corinthians 12:7).

You must never treat a cancer case as anything else but a living, evil spirit that is destroying the body. It is one of the worst kinds of evil spirits I know. Not that the devil has anything good—every disease of the devil is bad, either to a greater or lesser degree—but this form of disease is one that you must cast out. In casting out demons, we have to be careful about who gives the command. Man may say, "Come out," but unless his command is by the Spirit of God, man's words are useless.

You must be sure of your ground; you must be sure that there is a power mightier than you that is destroying the devil. Take your position from the first epistle of John and say, "*Greater is he that is in* [me], *than he that is in the world*" (1 John 4:4 KJV). If you think the power comes from you, you make a great mistake. It comes from your being filled with Him, from His acting in the place of you—your thoughts, your words, your all being used by the Spirit of God.

Thought for today: It is no mistake to declare yourself against the devil.

MINISTERING THE GIFTS OF HEALINGS, PART 3

To another gifts of healings by the same Spirit.
—1 Corinthians 12:9

Scripture reading: Psalm 32

I am never happier in the Lord than when I am in a bedroom with a sick person. I have had more revelations of the Lord's presence when I have ministered to the sick at their bedsides than at any other time. It is as your heart goes out to the needy ones in deep compassion that the Lord manifests His presence. You are able to discern their conditions. It is then that you know you must be filled with the Holy Spirit to deal with the conditions before you.

I was called at ten o'clock one night to pray for a young person who was dying of tuberculosis and whom the doctor had given up on. As I looked, I saw that unless God intervened, it would be impossible for her to live. I turned to the mother and said, "Well, Mother, you will have to go to bed." She said, "Oh, I have not had my clothes off for three weeks." I said to the daughters, "You will have to go to bed," but they did not want to go. It was the same with the son. I put on my overcoat and said, "Goodbye, I'm leaving." They said, "Oh, don't leave us." I said, "I can do nothing here." They said, "Oh, if you will stay, we will all go to bed."

I knew that God would not move in an atmosphere of mere natural sympathy and unbelief. They all went to bed, and I stayed, and that was surely a time as I knelt by that bed face-to-face with death and the devil. But God can change the hardest situation and make you know that He is almighty.

Then the fight came. It seemed as though the heavens were brass. I prayed from 11:00 p.m. to 3:30 a.m. I saw the glimmering light on the face of the sufferer and saw her pass away. The devil said, "Now you are done for. You have come from Bradford, and the girl has died on your hands." I said, "It can't be. God did not send me here for nothing. This is a time to change strength." I remembered the passage that said, *"Men always ought to pray and not lose heart"* (Luke 18:1). Death had taken place, but I knew that my God was all-powerful and that He who had split the Red Sea is just the same today. It was a time when I would not accept "no" and God said, "Yes."

I looked at the window and at that moment, the face of Jesus appeared. It seemed as though a million rays of light were coming from His face. As He looked at the one who had just passed away, the color came back to her face. She rolled over and fell asleep. Then I had a glorious time. In the morning, she woke early, put on a dressing gown, and walked to the piano. She started to play and to sing a wonderful song. The mother, the sister, and the brother all came down to listen. The Lord had intervened! He had restored her lungs, making them perfectly sound. Praise God!

Thought for today: After the Holy Spirit comes, you are in the place of command.

THE MINISTRY OF LONGSUFFERING

You, O Lord, are a God full of compassion, and gracious, longsuffer-ing and abundant in mercy and truth.
—Psalm 86:15

Scripture reading: Galatians 5:19–6:3

A fruit of the Spirit that must accompany the gifts of healings is long-suffering. The person who is persevering with God must always be ready with a word of comfort. If the sick one is in distress and helpless and does not see everything eye to eye with you, you must bear with him. Our Lord Jesus Christ was filled with compassion and lived and moved in a place of longsuffering, and we will have to get into this place if we are to help needy ones.

There are times when you pray for the sick, and you seem to be rough with them. But you are not dealing with a person; you are dealing with satanic forces that are binding the person. Your heart is full of love and compassion toward all; however, you are moved to a holy anger as you see the place the devil has taken in the sick one, and you deal with the enemy with real forcefulness.

You are always right when you dare to deal with sickness as with the devil. Much sickness is caused by some misconduct; there is something wrong somewhere, and Satan has had a chance to get in. It is necessary to repent and confess where you have given place to the devil (Ephesians 4:27), and then he can be dealt with. It is our privilege in the power of the Holy Spirit to loose the prisoners of Satan and to let the oppressed go free.

Take your position from the first epistle of John and declare, *"He who is in [me] is greater than he who is in the world"* (1 John 4:4). Then recognize that it is not you who has to deal with the power of the devil, but the greater One who is in you. Oh, what it means to be filled with Him! You can do nothing in yourself, but He who is in you will win the victory. Your being has become the temple of the Holy Spirit. Your mouth, your mind, your whole being may be used and worked upon by the Spirit of God.

We need to wake up and strive to believe God. Before God could bring me to this place, He broke me a thousand times. I have wept; I have groaned; I have travailed many a night until God broke me. We will never have the gifts of healings and the working of miracles in operation unless we stand in the divine power that God gives us, unless we stand believing God and *"having done all"* (Ephesians 6:13), we still stand believing.

We have been seeing wonderful miracles, and they are only a little of what we are going to see. I believe that we are right on the threshold of wonderful things, but I want to emphasize that all these things will be only through the power of the Holy Spirit. You must not think that these gifts will fall upon you like ripe cherries. There is a sense in which you have to pay the price for everything you get. We must earnestly desire God's best gifts and say *amen* to any preparation the Lord takes us through. In this way, we will be humble, usable vessels through whom He Himself can operate by means of the Spirit's power.

Thought for today: It seems to me that until God has mowed you down, you can never have this longsuffering for others.

RESURRECTION LIFE

[Paul] is a chosen vessel of Mine to bear My name before Gentiles,
kings, and the children of Israel. For I will show him how many things
he must suffer for My name's sake.
—Acts 9:15–16

Scripture reading: Acts 20:7–12, 17–38

Paul preached from evening to midnight, and in the middle of the night, something startling happened. If you turn to Philippians, you will see a wonderful truth there where Paul says, *"I may attain to the resurrection"* (Philippians 3:11). Hear the words spoken to Martha, that wonderful saying when Jesus said to her, *"I am the resurrection and the life. He who believes in Me, though he may die, he shall live"* (John 11:25).

Paul desired to attain resurrection life, and it is remarkable evidence to me that you never attain anything until opportunity comes. On the activity of faith, you will find that God will bring so many things before your notice that you will have no time to think over them. You will jump into them and bring authority by the power of the Spirit. If you took time to think, you would miss the opportunity.

Likewise, you will find out that with the baptism of the Holy Spirit, you will be in a position where you must act because you have no time to think. The Holy Spirit works on the power of divine origin. It is the supernatural, God filling until it becomes a freeing power by the authority of the Almighty. It sees things come to pass that could not come to pass in any other way.

This is the position Paul found himself in. We read it in the account of Acts 20:9–12. It is midnight, and Paul has been preaching for hours. Death comes to a young man who falls asleep and falls from a window.

The first thing Paul does is the most absurd thing to do, yet it is the most practical thing to do in the Holy Spirit: he fell on the young man. Yes, fell on him, embraced him, and left him alive. *"And they brought the young man in alive, and they were not a little comforted"* (Acts 20:12). Some would say Paul fell on him, crushed Holy Spirit life into him, and brought him back. It is the activity of the Almighty.

We must see that in any meeting, the Holy Spirit can demonstrate His divine power until we realize that we are in the presence of God. All can be healed, where the power of the resurrection of Jesus Christ is clearly in evidence, where we see nothing but Jesus.

Thought for today: This same Jesus, in resurrection power, is present today.

OVERCOME IN JESUS'S NAME

Therefore God also has highly exalted Him and given Him
the name which is above every name,
that at the name of Jesus every knee should bow.
—Philippians 2:9–10

Scripture reading: Philippians 2:1–13

There is power to overcome everything in the world through the name of Jesus. *"There is no other name under heaven given among men by which we must be saved"* (Acts 4:12).

Six people went into the house of a sick man to pray for him. He was a leader in the Episcopal Church, and he lay in his bed utterly helpless. He had read a little tract about healing and had heard about people praying for the sick. So he sent for these friends; he thought they could pray *"the prayer of faith"* (James 5:15). He was anointed according to James 5:14, but because he had no immediate manifestation of healing, he wept bitterly. The six people walked out of the room, somewhat crestfallen to see the man lying there in an unchanged condition.

When they were outside, one of the six said, "There is one thing we could have done. I wish you would all go back with me and try it." They all went back and got together in a group. This brother said, "Let us whisper the name of Jesus."

At first, when they whispered this worthy name, nothing seemed to happen. But as they continued to whisper, "Jesus! Jesus! Jesus!" the power began to fall. As they saw that God was beginning to work, their faith and joy increased, and they spoke the name louder and louder. As they did so, the man rose from his bed and dressed himself.

The secret was just this: those six people had gotten their eyes off the sick man and were taken up with the Lord Jesus Himself. Their faith grasped the power in His name. Oh, if people would only appreciate the power in His name, there is no telling what would happen.

You cannot repeat the name of Jesus too often. What a privilege it is to kneel and get right into heaven the moment we pray, where the glory descends, the fire burns, faith is active, and the light dispels the darkness.

Jesus is the light and the life of men; no man can have this light and still walk in darkness (John 8:12). *"When Christ who is our life appears, then you also will appear with Him in glory"* (Colossians 3:4). Where His life is, disease cannot remain. Is not He who dwells in us greater than all? Is He greater? Yes, when He has full control. If one thing is permitted outside the will of God, it hinders us in our standing against the powers of Satan. We must allow the Word of God to judge us, lest we stand condemned with the world (1 Corinthians 11:32).

Thought for today: Through the name of Jesus and through the power of His name, we have access to God.

OH, THE NAME OF JESUS

As many as touched [His garment] *were made perfectly well.*
—Matthew 14:36

Scripture reading: Matthew 14:23–36

Oh, this life in the Holy Spirit! Oh, this life of deep inward revelation, of transformation from one state to another, of growing in grace, in all knowledge, and in the power of the Spirit! In this state, the life and the mind of Christ are renewed in you, and He gives constant revelations of the might of His power. In this life, the Lord puts you in all sorts of places and then reveals His power.

I had been preaching in New York, and one day I sailed for England on the *Lusitania*. As soon as I got on board, I went down to my cabin. Two men were there, and one of them said, "Well, will I do for company?" He took out a bottle and poured a glass of whiskey and drank it, and then he filled it up for me. "I never touch that stuff," I said. "How can you live without it?" he asked. "How could I live with it?" I replied.

"I have been under the influence of this stuff for months," he admitted, "and they say my insides are all shriveled up. I know that I am dying. I wish I could be delivered, but I just have to keep on drinking. Oh, if I could only be delivered! My father died in England and has given me his fortune, but what good will it be to me except to hasten me to my grave?"

I said to this man, "Say the word, and you will be delivered." He asked, "What do you mean?" I said, "Say the word—show that you are willing to be delivered—and God will deliver you." But it was just as if I were talking to a board for all the understanding he showed. So I said to him, "Stand still," and I laid my hands on his head in the name of Jesus and cursed that alcohol demon that was taking his life. He cried out, "I'm free! I'm free! I know I'm free!" He took two bottles of whiskey and threw them overboard, and God saved, sobered, and healed him.

I continued to preach all the way across the ocean. He sat beside me at the table. Prior to this, he had not been able to eat, but now at every meal he went right through the menu.

Oh, the name of Jesus! We make too little use of that name. Even the children cried, *"Hosanna"* (Matthew 21:15). If we would let ourselves go and praise Him more and more, God would give us the shout of victory.

You need only a touch from Jesus to have a good time. The power of God is just the same today. To me, He's lovely. To me, He's saving health. To me, He's the Lily of the Valley. Oh, this blessed Nazarene, this King of Kings! Hallelujah! Will you let Him have your will? Will you let Him have you? If so, all His power is at your disposal.

Thought for today: There is always a place of deliverance when you let God search out what is spoiling and marring your life.

RAISING LAZARUS, PART 1

The LORD will guide you continually.
—Isaiah 58:11

Scripture reading: Isaiah 58:1–14

One day while in Wales, I went up onto a mountain to pray. As I spent the day in the presence of the Lord, His Holy Spirit seemed to envelop and saturate me.

Two years before this time, two young men from Wales had come to our house. They were just ordinary lads, but they became very zealous for God. They came to our mission and saw some of the works of God. They said to me, "We would not be surprised if the Lord brings you down to Wales to raise our Lazarus." They explained that the leader of their church was a man named Lazarus who had spent his days working in a tin mine and his nights preaching. The result was that he had collapsed and contracted tuberculosis. For four years he had been a helpless invalid, having to be fed by others.

As I was on the mountaintop that day, the Lord said to me, "I want you to go and raise Lazarus." I told the brother who had accompanied me about this word from the Lord, and when we got down to the valley, I wrote a postcard. It read, "When I was up on the mountain praying today, God told me that I was to go and raise Lazarus." My friend went with me. When we arrived at the place, we went to the man to whom I had addressed the postcard. He looked at me and asked, "Did you send this?" "Yes," I replied. He said, "Do you think we believe in this? Here, take it." And he threw the card at me.

The man called a servant and said, "Take this man and show him Lazarus." Then he said to me, "The moment you see him, you will be ready to go home. Nothing will keep you here." Everything he said was true from a human standpoint. The man was helpless. He was nothing but a mass of bones with skin stretched over them. There was no life to be seen. Everything in him spoke of decay.

I said to him, "Will you shout? You remember that at Jericho, the people shouted while the walls were still up. God has a similar victory for you if you will only believe." But I could not get him to believe. There was not an atom of faith there.

It is a blessed thing to learn that God's Word can never fail. Never listen to human plans. God can work mightily when you persist in believing Him in spite of discouragement from the human standpoint. When I got back to the man to whom I had sent the postcard, he asked, "Are you ready to go now?" I replied, "I am not moved by what I see. I am moved only by what I believe. I know this: no man looks at the circumstances or relies on his feelings if he believes. The man who believes God has his request."

Thought for today: It will never do to give way to human opinions. If God says a thing, you have to believe Him.

RAISING LAZARUS, PART 2

The LORD will guide you continually.
—Isaiah 58:11

Scripture reading: Isaiah 59:1–2, 16–21

There were difficult conditions in that Welsh village where Lazarus lived, and it seemed impossible to get the people to believe. "Ready to go home?" I was asked again. But a man and a woman there asked us to come and stay with them. So, my friend and I stayed.

I said to the people in the village, "I want to know how many of you people can pray." No one wanted to pray. I asked if I could get seven people to pray for the poor man's deliverance. I said to the two people we were to stay with, "I will count on you two, and there is my friend and myself. We need three others." I told the people that I trusted that some of them would awaken to their privilege and come in the morning and join us in prayer for the raising of Lazarus from his bed.

I also told them that I would not eat anything that night as I went to the Lord in prayer. When I got to bed, it seemed as if the devil tried to place on me everything that he had placed on that poor man on the sickbed. When I awoke in the middle of the night, I had a cough and all the weakness of a man with tuberculosis. I rolled out of bed onto the floor and cried out to God to deliver me from the power of the devil. I shouted loud enough to wake everybody in the house, but nobody was disturbed. The Holy Spirit gave the victory, and I got back into bed again as free as I had ever been in my life.

At five o'clock in the morning, the Lord awakened me and said, "Don't break bread until you break it around My table." At six o'clock, He gave me these words: *"And I will raise him up"* (John 6:40). I elbowed the fellow who was sleeping in the same room. He said, "Ugh!" I elbowed him again and said, "Do you hear? The Lord says that He will raise him up."

At eight o'clock, my hosts said to me, "Have a little refreshment." But I have found prayer and fasting the greatest joy, and you will always find it so when you are led by God's Spirit. When we went to the house where Lazarus lived, there were eight of us altogether. God had laid it on the heart of four others to join us.

No one can prove to me that God does not always answer prayer. He always does more than that. He gives *"exceedingly abundantly above all that we ask or think"* (Ephesians 3:20).

Thought for today: The living God has chosen us for His divine inheritance, and it is He who is preparing us for our ministry, so that it may be of God and not of man.

RAISING LAZARUS, PART 3

The LORD will guide you continually.
—Isaiah 58:11

Scripture reading: Psalm 119:105

I will never forget how the power of God fell on us as we walked into Lazarus's sick room.

As we made a circle around the bed, I got one brother to hold the sick man's hand on one side, and I held the other, and we each held the hand of the person next to us. I said, "We are not going to pray; we are just going to use the name of Jesus." We all knelt down and whispered that one word, *"Jesus! Jesus! Jesus!"* The power of God fell, and then it lifted.

Five times, the power of God fell, and then it remained. But the man in the bed was unmoved. Two years previously, someone had come along and had tried to raise him up, and the devil had used his lack of success as a means of discouraging Lazarus. I said, "I don't care what the devil says. If God says He will raise you up, it must be so. Forget everything else except what God says about Jesus."

A sixth time the Holy Spirit's power fell, and the sick man's lips began moving, and the tears began to fall. I said to him, "The power of God is here; it is yours to accept." He answered, "I have been bitter in my heart, and I know I have grieved the Spirit of God. Here I am, helpless. I cannot raise my hands or even lift a spoon to my mouth."

I answered him, "Repent, and God will hear you." He repented and cried out, "Oh, God, let this be to Your glory." As he said these words, the power of the Lord went right through him.

I have asked the Lord to let me never tell this story except the way it happened, for I realize that God can never bless exaggerations. As we again said, *"Jesus! Jesus! Jesus!"* the bed shook, and the man shook. I said to the people who were with me, "You can all go downstairs now. This is all God. I'm not going to assist him." I sat and watched that man get up and dress himself. We sang the doxology as he walked down the steps. I said to him, "Now tell everyone what has happened."

It was soon told everywhere that Lazarus had been raised up. People came from all over to see him and to hear his testimony. God brought salvation to many. Right out in the open air, this man told what God had done, and as a result, many were convicted and converted. All this occurred through the name of Jesus, *"through faith in His name"* (Acts 3:16). Yes, the faith that comes by believing in Jesus gave this sick man perfect soundness in the presence of them all.

Thought for today: You must have an activity of faith, refusing the conditions in the name of Jesus.

"GOD HAS REVEALED JESUS TO ME"

And suddenly a voice came from heaven, saying, "This is My beloved Son, in whom I am well pleased."
—Matthew 3:17

Scripture reading: Matthew 3:13–17

I was preaching one day about the name of Jesus, and there was a man leaning against a lamppost, listening. He needed the lamppost to enable him to stay on his feet. I asked him, "Are you sick?" He showed me his hand, and I saw that inside his coat he had a silver-handled dagger. He told me that he had been on his way to kill his unfaithful wife but that he had heard me speaking about the power of the name of Jesus and could not get away. He said he felt helpless. I said, "Kneel down." There on the square, with people passing back and forth, he got saved.

I took him to my home and clothed him with a new suit. I saw something in that man that God could use. He said to me the next morning, "God has revealed Jesus to me. I see that all has been laid upon Jesus." I lent him some money, and he soon prepared a wonderful little home. His faithless wife was living with another man, but he invited her back to the home that he had for her. She came. Where enmity and hatred had been before, the whole situation was transformed by love. God made that man a minister wherever he went. Everywhere there is power in the name of Jesus. God can *"save to the uttermost"* (Hebrews 7:25).

Another miraculous healing took place in Stockholm. There was a home for incurables there, and one of the patients was brought to the meeting. He had palsy and was shaking all over. In front of three thousand people, he came to the platform, supported by two others. The power of

God fell on him as I anointed him in the name of Jesus. The moment I touched him, he dropped his crutch and began to walk in the name of Jesus. He walked around that great building in view of all the people.

I dropped into a shoemaker's shop one morning, and there was a man who had his eyes covered with a green shade. They were so inflamed that he was suffering terribly. He said, "I cannot rest anywhere." I did not ask him what he believed but laid down my Bible and put my hands on those poor suffering eyes and prayed, "In the name of Jesus." He said, "This is strange; I have no pain. I am free."

Do you think the human mind can do that? I say, "No." We do these things with a consciousness that God will answer, and He is pleased with that kind of service.

Thought for today: There is nothing that our God cannot do. He will do everything if you will dare to believe.

"RISE UP AND WALK"

Silver and gold I do not have, but what I do have I give you: In the name of Jesus Christ of Nazareth, rise up and walk.
—Acts 3:6

Scripture reading: Acts 3:1–16

Peter and John were helpless and uneducated. They had no college education; they had only some training in fishing. But they had been with Jesus. To them had come a wonderful revelation of the power of the name of Jesus. They had handed out the bread and fish after Jesus had multiplied them. They had sat at the table with Him, and John had often gazed into His face. Jesus often had had to rebuke Peter, but He had manifested His love to him through it all. Yes, He loved Peter, the wayward one.

Oh, He's a loving Savior! I have been wayward and stubborn. I had an unmanageable temper at one time, but how patient He has been. I am here to tell you that there is power in Jesus and in His wondrous name to transform anyone, to heal anyone.

If only you will see Him as God's Lamb, as God's beloved Son, upon whom was laid *"the iniquity of us all"* (Isaiah 53:6). If only you will see that Jesus paid the whole price for our redemption so that we might be free. Then you can enter into your purchased inheritance of salvation, of life, and of power.

Poor Peter and John! They had no money. I don't think there are many who are as poor as Peter and John were. But they had faith; they had the power of the Holy Spirit; they had God…and they had the name of Jesus!

And a certain man lame from his mother's womb was carried, whom they laid daily at the gate of the temple which is called Beautiful, to ask alms from those who entered the temple; who, seeing Peter and John about to go into the temple, asked for alms. And fixing his eyes on him, with John, Peter said, "Look at us." So he gave them his attention, expecting to receive something from them. Then Peter said, "Silver and gold I do not have, but what I do have I give you: In the name of Jesus Christ of Nazareth, rise up and walk." And he took him by the right hand and lifted him up, and immediately his feet and ankle bones received strength. So he, leaping up, stood and walked and entered the temple with them—walking, leaping, and praising God. (Acts 3:2–8)

You can have God even though you have nothing else. Even if you have lost your character, you can have God. I have seen the worst men saved by the power of God.

Thought for today: When you are in weakness, God will be with you in might. Everything that seems weak from a human perspective will be under the control of divine power.

WHO ARE YOU?

Jesus I know, and Paul I know; but who are you?
—Acts 19:15

Scripture reading: Isaiah 42:1–13

Paul did not have any power of his own that enabled him to use the name of Jesus as he did over evil spirits. But when he had to go through the privations and the difficulties, and even when all things seemed as if they were shipwrecked, God stood by him and caused him to know that there was Someone with him, supporting him all the time, Someone who was able to carry him through and bring out what his heart was longing for all the time. He seemed to be so unconsciously filled with the Holy Spirit that all that was needed was to bring the aprons and the handkerchiefs to him and then send them forth to heal and deliver.

I can imagine those itinerant Jewish exorcists and those seven sons of Sceva in the city of Ephesus looking on and seeing Paul and saying, "The power seems to be all in that name. Don't you notice that when he sends out the handkerchiefs and the aprons, he says, 'In the name of the Lord Jesus, I command the evil spirit to come out'?" (Acts 19).

These people had been watching, and they thought, "It is only the name; that is all that is needed," and so they said, "We will do the same."

They were determined to make this thing work, and they came to a man who was possessed with an evil power. As they entered into the house where he was, they said, "*We charge you in the name of Jesus, whom Paul preaches, to come out.*" The demon said, "*Jesus I know, and Paul I know; but who are you?*" (Acts 19:15). Then the evil power leaped upon them and tore their clothes off their backs, and they went out naked and wounded.

Oh, that God would help us to understand the name of Jesus! There is something in that name that attracts the whole world. It is the name, oh, it is still the name, but you must understand that there is the ministry of the name. It is the Holy Spirit who is behind the ministry. The power is in knowing Jesus Christ through the Holy Spirit.

Jesus is equal to every occasion. He is waiting for an opportunity to bless. He is ready for every opportunity to deliver souls. When we receive Jesus, the following verse is true of us, *"Greater is he that is in* [us], *than he that is in the world"* (1 John 4:4 KJV). He is greater than all the powers of darkness. No one can meet the devil in his own strength, but anyone filled with the knowledge of Jesus, filled with His presence, filled with His power, is more than a match for the powers of darkness. God has called us to be *"more than conquerors through Him who loved us"* (Romans 8:37).

God is compassionate and says, *"Seek the Lord while He may be found"* (Isaiah 55:6). He has further stated, *"Whoever calls on the name of the Lord shall be saved"* (Acts 2:21). Seek Him now; call on His name right now. There is forgiveness, healing, redemption, and deliverance—everything you need right here and now, and that which will satisfy you throughout eternity.

Thought for today: The name of Jesus brings power over the enemies of darkness.

DON'T MISTAKE THE POWER

There is no other name under heaven given among
men by which we must be saved.
—Acts 4:12

Scripture reading: Acts 19:13–20

I implore you in the name of Jesus, especially those of you who are baptized in the Holy Spirit, to wake up to the fact that you have power if God is with you. But there must be a resemblance between you and Jesus.

Paul had the resemblance. You are not going to get this resemblance without having His presence; His presence changes you. You are not going to be able to get the results without the marks of the Lord Jesus. You must have the divine power within yourself; devils will take no notice of any power if they do not see Christ. Remember what we read in Acts 19:15, when the evil spirit said, *"Jesus I know, and Paul I know; but who are you?"* The difference in these exorcists was that they did not have the marks of Christ, so the manifestation of the power of Christ was not seen.

If you want power, don't make any mistakes about it. If you speak in tongues, don't mistake that for the power. If God has given you revelations along certain lines, don't mistake that for the power. Or if you have even laid hands on the sick and they have been healed, don't mistake that for the power. *"The Spirit of the LORD is upon Me"* (Luke 4:18)—that alone is the power. It is the sense of the Holy Spirit, the knowledge of His power, the sweetness of His experience, the wonder of His presence, honoring the Word, making all new, meeting the present need.

Don't be deceived. There is a place to be reached where you know the Holy Spirit is upon you so that you will be able to do the works that are accomplished by this blessed Spirit of God in you. Then the manifestation of His power will be seen, and people will believe in the Lord.

God wants us to be ministering spirits, and this means being clothed with another power. You know when this divine power is there, and you know when it goes forth. Beloved, we can reach it; it is a high mark, but we can get to it.

Do you ask how? Say to God, *"What do You want me to do?"* (Acts 9:6). That is the plan. It means a perfect surrender to the call of God and perfect obedience.

Thought for today: The baptism of the Holy Spirit must bring us to the place of having our focus centered on the glory of God; everything else is wasted time and wasted energy.

IS ANYONE SICK?

They brought to Him many who were demon-possessed. And He
cast out the spirits with a word, and healed all who were sick, that it
might be fulfilled which was spoken by Isaiah the prophet, saying: "He
Himself took our infirmities and bore our sicknesses."
—Matthew 8:16–17

Scripture reading: Matthew 25:14–46

"Is there anyone sick in this place?" This is what I ask when I go into a sickroom. Why? I will tell you a story that will explain.

My daughter is a missionary to Africa. I am interested in helping to support missionaries in Africa and all over. I love missionary work.

We had a missionary out in China who by some means or other got rheumatism. I have no word for rheumatism. Rheumatism, cancer, tumors, lumbago, neuralgia—all these things I give only one name: the power of the devil working in humanity. All these things can be removed.

When Jesus went into Peter's house, where his wife's mother lay sick, what did He do? Did He cover her up with a blanket and put a hot water bottle on her feet? If He didn't do that, why didn't He? Because He knew that the demons had all the heat of hell in them. He did the right thing: He rebuked the fever, and it left (Luke 4:38–39). We, too, ought to do the right thing with these diseases.

This missionary came home to Belfast from China, enraged against the work of God, enraged against God, enraged against everything. She was absolutely outside the plan of God.

On the day that I was to visit the sick, she asked me to come. When I went to her room, I looked at her and called out, "Is there anyone sick in this room?" No response. "Is there anyone sick in this room?" No response. "Well," I said, "we will wait until somebody responds."

By and by, she said, "Yes, I am sick." I said, "All right, we have found you out then. You are in the room. Now the Word of God says that when you are sick, you are to pray. When you pray, I will anoint you and pray for you, but not before."

It took her almost a quarter of an hour to yield, the devil had such possession of her. But thank God, she yielded. Then she cried and cried, and by the power of God, her body was shaken loose, and she was set free. This happened when she repented and not before.

Oh, what would happen if everybody would repent! Talk about blessings! The glory would fall. We need to see that God wants us to be blessed, but first of all, He wants us to be ready for the blessing.

God wants you to have a living faith; He wants you to possess a vital touch, shaking the foundation of all weakness. When you were saved, you were saved the moment you believed, and you will be healed the moment you believe. If you believe, you can be healed. God means for you to believe today. God means for you to be helped today.

Thought for today: God's Word can bring things to pass today as it did in the past.

JESUS IS THE ROCK

Assuredly, I say to you, whatever you bind on earth will be bound in heaven, and whatever you loose on earth will be loosed in heaven.
—Matthew 18:18

Scripture reading: Psalm 18:1-3

Beloved, we are now living in the understanding that Jesus Christ is the Rock. I am glad, for we are within reach of wonderful possibilities because of the Rock. Take a stand on the fact that the Rock cannot be overthrown.

A man brought his son to my meeting, and he was all drawn to one side from having fits for years. The father asked, "Can you do anything for my son?" I said in the name of Jesus, "Yes, he can be healed." I knew it could be done because of the Rock. There is a Spirit who dwells within us, and He is nothing less than the life of Him who gave Himself for us, for He is the life of the Rock in us.

I wonder if you are waiting until some mighty power sweeps over you before you feel you have power to bind and loose. That is not the power. The Rock is within you; you have power to bind and power to loose because you consist of the Rock. What you must do is stand on that fact and use the power. Will you do it?

I said, "Father, in the name of Jesus, I bind the evil spirit in this young man."

The father brought the young man to the next meeting, and I did not need to ask if he was delivered. The brightness of his face and the shining of the father's face told the story. But I asked, "Is he all right now?" and he said, "Yes."

Oh, I see it is needed so much, this *power to bind and power to loose.*

Brothers and sisters, wherever you are, you can set people free. God wants to change your name from Doubting Thomas to Prevailing Israel. Will you use the power of the Rock for His glory?

A young woman who had cancer was brought to me. Her spirits were very low. People need to be made glad. I said to her, "Cheer up," but I could not get her to cheer up. So I bound the evil power in the name of Jesus and then laid my hands on her and said, "Sister, you are free." She arose and asked if she could say something. She rubbed the place where the cancer had been and said, "It is all gone!"

Oh, brothers and sisters, I want you to see that that power is yours. I believe every child of God has a measure of this power, but there is a fuller manifestation of the power when we get so filled that we speak in tongues. I want you to press on until you get the fullness.

When will we see all the people filled with the Holy Spirit and things done as they were in the Acts of the apostles? It will be when all the people say, "Lord, You are God." I want you to come into a place of such relationship with God that you will know your prayers are answered because He has promised.

Thought for today: God is delighted when we use the power He has given us.

KEPT BY GOD'S POWER

While I was with them in the world, I kept them in Your name.
Those whom You gave Me I have kept.
—John 17:12

Scripture reading: John 17

There are evil powers, but Jesus is greater than all evil powers. There are tremendous diseases, but Jesus is the Healer. No case is too hard for Him. The Lion of Judah will break every chain. He came to relieve the oppressed and set the captive free (Luke 4:18). He came to bring redemption, to make us as perfect as man was before the fall.

Praise God, this same Jesus also said, *"I have power to lay [My life] down, and I have power to take it again"* (John 10:18). He can make us overcomers by dwelling in us by His mighty power and destroying the power of sin. He can transform us until we *"love righteousness and hate wickedness"* (Psalm 45:7), so that we can be holy.

People want to know how to be kept by the power of God. He will contend for your body. When you are saved, Satan will come around and say, "See, you are not saved." The devil is a liar. Jesus comes to help you as *"the way, the truth, and the life"* (John 14:6).

I remember the story of the man whose life was swept and put in order. The evil power had been swept out of him. But the man was not filled with the Holy Spirit. If the Lord heals you, you dare not remain unresponsive to His Spirit. The evil spirit came back to that man, found his house swept, and took seven others worse than himself and dwelt there. The last stage of that man was worse than the first (Matthew 12:43–45). Be sure to get filled with God. Get an Occupier. Be filled with the Spirit.

God's power cannot come out of you unless it is within you. We must have all inward confidence and knowledge that we are God's property, bought and paid for by the precious blood of Jesus. God wants you to know how to claim the victory and shout in the face of the devil and say, "Lord, it is done" (Revelation 21:6).

God has a million ways of undertaking for those who go to Him for help. He has deliverance for every captive. He loves you so much that He even says, *"Before they call, I will answer"* (Isaiah 65:24). Don't turn Him away.

Thought for today: Every position of grace into which you are led—forgiveness, healing, any kind of deliverance—will be contested by Satan. But Jesus's power is greater.

LOOKING FOR THE MESSIAH

Are You the Coming One, or do we look for another?
—Matthew 11:3

Scripture reading: Matthew 11:12–24

I want you to see how satanic power can work in the mind. Satan came to John the Baptist when he was in prison. I find that Satan can come to any of us.

But I want to prove that we have a greater power than Satan's—in imagination, in thought, in everything. Satan came to John the Baptist in prison and said to him, "Don't you think you have made a mistake? Here you are in prison. Isn't there something wrong with the whole business? After all, you may be greatly deceived about being a forerunner of the Christ."

I find men who might be giants of faith, who might be leaders of society, who might rise to subdue kingdoms (Hebrews 11:33), who might be noble among princes, but they are defeated because they allow the suggestions of Satan to dethrone their better knowledge of the power of God. May God help us.

John sent two of his disciples to ask Jesus, "Are You the Messiah?" How could Jesus send those men back with a stimulating truth, with a personal, effective power that would stir their hearts to know that they had met Him about whom all the prophets had spoken? What would declare it? How would they know? How could they tell it?

Jesus answered and said to them, "Go and tell John the things which you hear and see: the blind see and the lame walk; the lepers are cleansed and the deaf hear; the dead are raised up and the poor have the gospel preached to them." (Matthew 11:4–5)

And when they saw the miracles and wonders and heard the gracious words He spoke as the power of God rested upon Him, they were ready to believe.

I come across people everywhere I go who are held bound by deceptive conditions, and these conditions have come about simply because they have allowed the devil to make their minds the place of his stronghold. How are we to guard against this? The Lord has provided us with weapons that are mighty through God for the pulling down of these strongholds of the enemy (2 Corinthians 10:4), by means of which every thought will be brought "*into captivity to the obedience of Christ*" (v. 5). Jesus's blood and His mighty name are an antidote to all the subtle seeds of unbelief that Satan would sow in your mind.

Thought for today: You must be filled, or divinely insulated, with the power of God, so that you are not deceived by the power of Satan.

WORDS OF WISDOM

"Your adversary the devil walks about like a roaring lion, seeking whom he may devour. Resist him, steadfast in the faith."
—1 Peter 5:8–9

Scripture reading: 1 Peter 5:1–11

Let's take a look at the fifth chapter of 1 Peter, which is full of wisdom. *"Humble yourselves"* (v. 6). Look at the Master at the Jordan River, submitting Himself to the baptism of John, then again submitting Himself to the cruel cross. Truly, angels desire to look into these things (1 Peter 1:12), and all heaven is waiting for the man who will burn all the bridges behind him and allow God to begin a plan in righteousness, so full, so sublime, beyond all human thought, but according to the revelation of the Spirit.

"Casting all your care upon Him, for He cares for you" (1 Peter 5:7). He cares! We sometimes forget this. If we descend into the natural, all goes wrong, but when we trust Him and abide beneath His shadow, how blessed it is. Oh, many times I have experienced my helplessness and nothingness, and casting my care upon Him has proved that He cares.

Verse eight tells us to *"be sober, be vigilant."* What does it mean to be sober? It means to have a clear knowledge that we are powerless to manage, but also to have a rest of faith. The adversary's opportunity is when we think that we are something and try to open our own door. Our thoughts, words, and deeds must all be in the power of the Holy Spirit. Oh yes, we need to be sober—not only sober, but also vigilant. We need not only to be filled with the Holy Spirit but also to have a "go forth" in us, a knowledge that God's holy presence is with us. To be sober and vigilant, to have an ability to judge, discern, and balance things that differ—this is what we need.

"*Your adversary the devil walks about like a roaring lion, seeking whom he may devour. Resist him, steadfast in the faith*" (1 Peter 5:8–9). We must resist in the hour when Satan's schemes may bewilder us, when we are almost swept off our feet, and when darkness is upon us to such a degree that it seems as if some evil thing had overtaken us. "*Resist him, steadfast in the faith.*"

"*He who keeps Israel shall neither slumber nor sleep*" (Psalm 121:4). God covers us, for no human can stand against the powers of hell.

"*After you have suffered a while*" (1 Peter 5:10). Then there is some suffering? Yes! But it is "*not worthy to be compared with the glory which shall be revealed in us*" (Romans 8:18). The difference is so great that our suffering is not even worthy of mention. Ours is an eternal glory, from glory to glory, until we are swallowed up, until we are swallowed up in Him, the Lord of glory.

Thought for today: God is close at hand to deliver all the time.

CHRIST'S WORK CONTINUES

Your healing shall spring forth speedily.
—Isaiah 58:8

Scripture reading: Jeremiah 33:3–16

The ministry of Christ did not end at the cross. Our blessed Lord Jesus is still alive and continues His ministry through those who are filled with His Spirit. He is still healing the brokenhearted and delivering the captives through those on whom He places His Spirit.

I was traveling on a train in Sweden. At one station, an old lady boarded with her daughter. That old lady's expression was so troubled that I asked her what the matter was. I heard that she was going to the hospital to have her leg amputated. She began to weep as she told me that the doctors had said that there was no hope for her except through having her leg amputated. I said to my interpreter, "Tell her that Jesus can heal her." The instant these words were said to her, it was as though a veil had been taken off her face; it became so radiant.

We stopped at another station, and the train filled up with people. A large group of men rushed to board the train, and the devil said, "You're done." But I knew I had the best situation. Hard things are always opportunities to gain more glory for the Lord as He manifests His power.

Every trial is a blessing. There have been times when I have been hard-pressed through circumstances, and it seemed as if a dozen steamrollers were going over me, but we have such a lovely Jesus. He always proves Himself to be a mighty Deliverer. He never fails to plan the best things for us.

As the train began moving, I crouched down and in the name of Jesus commanded the disease to leave. The old lady cried in Swedish, "I'm healed!

I know I'm healed!" She stamped her leg and said, "I'm going to prove it." So when we stopped at another station, she marched up and down and shouted, "I'm not going to the hospital." Once again, our wonderful Jesus had proven Himself a Healer of the brokenhearted, a Deliverer of one who was bound.

At one meeting, there was a seventy-seven-year-old woman who was paralyzed. The power of God came into her, and she was so strengthened and blessed after prayer that she rushed up and down in a marvelous way.

Brothers and sisters, what I see in both of these women's healing is an illustration of what God will do. I am trusting that we will all be so strengthened today with the power of God that we will not allow any doubt or fear to come into our hearts. On the contrary, we will know that we are created anew by a living faith and that there is in that faith within us power to accomplish wonderful things for God.

Thought for today: The hardest circumstances are just lifting places into the grace of God.

THE POWER OF JESUS'S WORDS

Only speak a word, and my servant will be healed.
—Matthew 8:8

Scripture reading: Matthew 8:5–13

A centurion came to Jesus, pleading on behalf of his servant who was paralyzed and dreadfully tormented. This Roman officer was so earnest that he came seeking Jesus. Notice this certainty: there is no such thing as seeking without finding. *"He who seeks finds"* (Matthew 7:8). Listen to the gracious words of Jesus: *"I will come and heal him"* (Matthew 8:7). But the centurion said, *"Lord, I am not worthy that You should come under my roof. But only speak a word, and my servant will be healed"* (Matthew 8:8). Jesus was delighted with this expression and *"said to the centurion, 'Go your way; and as you have believed, so let it be done for you.' And his servant was healed that same hour"* (v. 13). The words Jesus spoke were enough.

In most places where I go, there are many people for whom I cannot pray. In some places, there are two or three hundred people who would like me to visit them, but I am not able to do so. Yet I am glad that the Lord Jesus is always willing to come and heal. He longs to heal them of their afflictions. The Lord is healing many people today by means of handkerchiefs, even as He did in the days of Paul (Acts 19:11–12).

A woman came to me in the city of Liverpool and said, "My husband is a drunkard, and every night, he comes into the home under the influence of alcohol. Won't you join me in prayer for him?" I asked the woman, "Do you have a handkerchief?" She took out a handkerchief, and I prayed over it and told her to lay it on her husband's pillow. He came home that night and laid his head on the pillow, but he laid his head on more than the pillow that night, for he laid his head on the promise of God. In Mark 11:24, we read, *"Whatever things you ask when you pray, believe that you receive them, and you will have them."*

The next morning, the man got up and going into the first saloon that he passed on his way to work, ordered some beer. He tasted it and said to the bartender, "You put some poison in this beer." He could not drink it and went on to the next saloon and ordered some more beer. He tasted it and said to the man behind the counter, "You put some poison in this beer. I believe you folks have plotted to poison me." The bartender was indignant at being charged with this crime. The man said, "I will go somewhere else." He went to another saloon, and the same thing happened. He made such a disturbance that he was thrown out.

He went home later and told his wife what had happened, "It seems as though all the fellows have agreed to poison me." His wife answered, "Can't you see the hand of the Lord in this, that He is making you dislike the stuff that has been your ruin?" This word brought conviction to the man's heart, and he came to the meeting and got saved. The Lord still has the power to set the captives free.

Thought for today: Jesus is equal to every occasion. There is power in the words of Jesus.

A GOOD FOUNDATION

Being rooted and grounded in love.
—Ephesians 3:17

Scripture reading: Ephesians 3:14–19

It is quite easy to construct a building if the foundation is secure. On the other hand, a building will be unstable if it does not have a solid understructure. Likewise, it is not very easy to rise spiritually unless we have a real spiritual power working within us. It will never do for us to be top-heavy—the base must always be very firmly set.

Many of us have not gone on in the Lord because we have not had a secure foundation in Him, and we will have to consider *"the pit from which* [we] *were dug"* (Isaiah 51:1). Unless we correctly understand the spiritual leadings, according to the mind of God, we will never be able to stand when the winds blow, when the trials come, and when Satan appears as *"an angel of light"* (2 Corinthians 11:14).

There must be three things in our lives if we wish to go all the way with God in the fullness of Pentecost. First, we must be grounded and settled in love. We must have a real knowledge of what love is: *"God, who is rich in mercy, because of His great love with which He loved us"* (Ephesians 2:4); *"to know the love of Christ which passes knowledge; that you may be filled with all the fullness of God"* (Ephesians 3:19).

Second, we must have a clear understanding of the Word, for love must manifest the Word. Third, we must clearly understand our own ground because it is our own ground that needs to be looked after the most.

The Lord speaks at least twice of the good ground into which seed was sown, which also bore fruit and brought forth some hundredfold, some sixty, and some thirty (Matthew 13:8; Mark 4:8). Even in the good ground, the seed yielded different portions of fruit. I maintain truly that there is no limitation to the abundance of a harvest when the ground is perfectly in the hands of the Lord. So we must clearly understand that the Word of God can never come forth with all its primary purposes unless our ground is right. But God will help us, I believe, to see that He can put the ground in perfect order as it is left in His hands.

Thought for today: We will never be able to stand unless we are firmly fixed in the Word of God.

SACRIFICE IS NOTHING WITHOUT LOVE

And though I bestow all my goods to feed the poor, and though I give
my body to be burned, but have not love, it profits me nothing.
—1 Corinthians 13:3

Scripture reading: Mark 6:30–56

Though I can lay my hands on millions of dollars, though I can do all kinds of things with the money, and though, after I have given it all, I show the people more by giving my body to be burned, saying, "I will show what I am made of!" this is nothing, nothing! Five dollars given in the name of the Lord is of more value than thousands without acknowledging Him.

A man came to me, and we had long talks about the Lord. He told me, "I was in a very difficult place. I had been working very hard in the church and had given all my strength."

Oh, I see such godly, holy people doing more than they ought to, thereby giving themselves away. Don't you know that your body belongs to God (1 Corinthians 6:19–20), and that, if you overtax your body, God says He will judge you for it? We have to be careful because the body that is given to us is to exhibit His power and His glory, and we cannot do this if we give ourselves all the time to work, work, work and think that that is the only way. It is not the way.

The Scriptures teach us that Jesus had to go and renew His spiritual vision and power in solitude with His Father (Mark 1:35), and it was also necessary for the disciples to draw aside and rest awhile (Mark 6:30–31). Couldn't Jesus give them all they needed? My dear brother, whatever God gives you, He will never take away your common sense.

Suppose I unwisely overextended my body and knew that I had done so? How could I ask anyone to pray for me unless I repented? We must be careful. Our bodies are the temples of the Holy Spirit, and He has to dwell in them, and they have to be for His purpose in the world. We are not working for ourselves; God is to be glorified in our bodies. Many today are absolutely withered up, years before their time, because they went beyond their knowledge.

Thought for today: Your gifts will perish unless the gifts are used for the glory of Jesus.

A MORE EXCELLENT WAY

Let everything that has breath praise the LORD. Praise the LORD!
—Psalm 150:6

Scripture reading: Psalm 150

If you ever get to the place where you cannot praise the Lord, it is a calamity in your life and it is a calamity to the people who are around you. If you want to take blessing into homes and make all the people around you know that you have something more than an ordinary life, you must know that God has come to supplant you and put within you a perfect praise.

God has a great place for us, so that His will may be done, and we may be subject to His perfect will. When that comes to pass, no one can tell what may happen, for Jesus reached the highest place when He said, *"For I have come down from heaven, not to do My own will, but the will of Him who sent Me"* (John 6:38). So there is something in a place of yielding where God can have us for His own.

God desires that we would lose ourselves in Him in a way we have never done before. I want to provoke you to love so that you will come into this place of blessing.

Beloved, believe today that God has a way for you. Perhaps you have never come that way before. God has a way beyond all your ways of thought. He has a plan for you.

There is a great need today. People are hungry for truth. People are thirsting, wanting to know God better. There are thousands *"in the valley of decision"* (Joel 3:14), wanting someone to take them right into the depths of God.

Are you ready to pray? You say, "What should I ask for?"

You may not know what to ask for, but if you begin, the Holy Spirit knows the desire of your heart, and He will pray according to the mind of God. You do not know, but God knows everything, and He is acquainted with you altogether and desires to promote you.

So I say, "Are you ready?" You say, "What for?" Are you ready to come promptly into the presence of God so that you may ask this day as you have never asked before? Ask in faith, doubting nothing, but believing that God is on the throne waiting to anoint you afresh today.

Are you ready? What for? Are you ready to be brought into the banquet house of God, even as Esther came in before King Ahasuerus? God will put out the scepter, and all that your heart desires He will give to you (Esther 5–7).

"Father, in Jesus's name we come before You believing in Your almightiness, that the power of Your hand does move us, chasten us. Build us. Let the Word of God sink into our hearts this day. Make us, oh God, worthy of the name we bear, that we may go about as real, holy saints of God. Just as if You were on the earth, fill us with Your anointing, Your power, and Your grace. Amen."

Thought for today: God wants you to be blessed so that you will be a blessing.

CHRIST IN US

There has not risen one greater than John the Baptist; but he who is
least in the kingdom of heaven is greater than he.
—Matthew 11:11

Scripture reading: Matthew 11:1–11

God wants to bring to us a living realization of what the Word of God is, what the Lord God means by what He says, and what we may expect if we believe it. I am certain that the Lord wishes to put before us a living fact that will, by our faith, bring into action a principle that is within our own hearts so that Christ can dethrone every power of Satan.

Only this truth revealed to our hearts can make us so much greater than we ever had any idea we could be. There is only the need of revelation and of stirring ourselves up to understand the mightiness that God has within us. We may prove what He has accomplished in us if we will only be willing to carry through what He has already accomplished in us.

For God has not accomplished something in us that should lie dormant, but He has brought within us a power, a revelation, a life that is so great that I believe God wants to reveal the greatness of it. There isn't anything you can imagine that is greater than what man may accomplish through Him.

But everything on a human basis is very limited compared with what God has for us on a spiritual basis. If man can accomplish much in a short time, what may we accomplish if we will believe the revealed Word and take it as truth that God has given us and that He wants to bring out in revelation and force?

Notice that John the Baptist was the forerunner of Jesus. Within his own short history, John the Baptist had the power of God revealed to him as probably no man in the old dispensation had. He had a wonderful revelation. He had a mighty anointing.

See how John moved Israel. See how the power of God rested upon him. See how he had the vision of Jesus and went forth with power and turned the hearts of Israel to Him. You, too, can do great things for God if you are a part of His kingdom!

> *Most assuredly, I say to you, he who believes in Me, the works that I do he will do also; and greater works than these he will do, because I go to My Father. And whatever you ask in My name, that I will do, that the Father may be glorified in the Son. If you ask anything in My name, I will do it.* (John 14:12–14)

Thought for today: Oh, the possibilities of man in the hands of God!

HOLINESS OPENS THE DOOR

*Grace and peace be multiplied to you in the knowledge of
God and of Jesus our Lord.*
—2 Peter 1:2

Scripture reading: 2 Peter 1:1–11

Note that grace and peace are multiplied through the knowledge of God, but first our faith comes through the righteousness of God. Righteousness comes first and knowledge afterwards. It cannot be otherwise. If you expect any revelation of God apart from holiness, you will have only a mixture. Holiness opens the door to all the treasures of God.

He must first bring us to the place where we, like our Lord, "[love] *righteousness* and [hate] *lawlessness*" (Hebrews 1:9), before He opens up to us these good treasures. When we *"regard iniquity in* [our hearts], *the Lord will not hear"* us (Psalm 66:18), and it is only as we are made righteous, pure, and holy through the precious blood of God's Son that we can enter into this life of holiness and righteousness in the Son. It is the righteousness of our Lord Himself made real in us as our faith remains in Him.

You must see that your life has to be clean, and that God will keep you holy. You must see that you have to walk before God and that He will make you perfect, for God says, *"Pursue…holiness, without which no one will see the Lord"* (Hebrews 12:14).

Oh, Jesus is lovely! Meditate on the beatitudes, the attributes, and the divine position Jesus manifested. This power of the new creation, this birth unto righteousness by faith in the atonement, can transform and change you until you are controlled, dominated, and filled with the Spirit of Jesus. Though you are still in the body, you are governed by the Spirit, with *"fruit to holiness, and the end, everlasting life"* (Romans 6:22).

After I was baptized with the Holy Spirit, the Lord gave me a blessed revelation. I saw Adam and Eve turned out of the garden for their disobedience. They were unable to partake of the Tree of Life, for the cherubim with flaming sword kept them away from this tree.

When I was baptized, I saw that I had begun to eat from this Tree of Life, and I saw that the flaming sword surrounded it. It was there to keep the devil away. How marvelously He keeps us so that the wicked one cannot touch us. I see a place in God where Satan cannot come. We are *"hidden with Christ in God"* (Colossians 3:3). He invites us all to come and share this wonderful hidden place. We dwell *"in the secret place of the Most High"* and *"abide under the shadow of the Almighty"* (Psalm 91:1).

Thought for today: We are saved, called with a holy calling—called to be saints, holy, pure, Godlike, sons with power.

A HUMBLE SPIRIT

On this one will I look: on him who is poor and of a contrite spirit.
—Isaiah 66:2

Scripture reading: Romans 2:1–16

One day I was in a meeting where there were a lot of doctors and eminent men and many ministers. The power of God fell on this meeting. A humble little girl who served as a waitress opened her heart to the Lord and was immediately filled with the Holy Spirit and began to speak in tongues. All these big men stretched their necks and looked up to see what was happening. They were saying, "Who is it?" Then they learned it was "the servant." Nobody received except the servant!

These things are hidden and kept back from the *"wise and prudent"* (Matthew 11:25), but the little children, the humble ones, are the ones who receive. We cannot have faith if we show undue deference to one another. A man who is going on with God won't accept honor from his fellow beings. God honors the person who has a broken, contrite spirit.

Oh, if I could only stir you up to see that, as you are faithful in the humblest role, God can fill you with His Spirit, make you a chosen vessel for Himself, and promote you to a place of mighty ministry in the salvation of souls and in the healing of the sick. Nothing is impossible to a man or woman filled with the Holy Spirit. The possibilities are beyond all human comprehension.

So many people want to do great things and to be seen doing them, but the one whom God will use is the one who is willing to be told what to do. And you and I will never do anything without compassion. We will never be able to remove the sickness until we are immersed so deeply in the power of the Holy Spirit that the compassion of Christ is moving through us.

I find that in everything my Lord did, He said that He did not do it but that another who was in Him did the work (John 14:10). What a holy submission! He was just an instrument for the glory of God. Have we reached a place where we dare to be trusted with a gift from God?

I see in 1 Corinthians 13 that if I have faith to move mountains and do not have love, all is a failure. When my love is so deepened in God that I only move for the glory of God, then the gifts can be made manifest. God wants to be manifested and to manifest His glory to those who are humble.

Thought for today: Let us move into the realm of faith, live in the realm of faith, and let God have His way.

KEEP YOUR MIND ON JESUS

You will keep him in perfect peace, whose mind is stayed on You,
because he trusts in You.
—Isaiah 26:3

Scripture reading: Isaiah 54:5–55:9

We must keep in the spiritual tide—God supreme, the altar within the body. Faith is the evidence, the power, the principle, keeping us in rest. We must have the Holy Spirit in anointing, intercession, revelation, and great power of ministry. To be baptized in the Holy Spirit is to be in God's plan—the Spirit preeminent, revealing the Christ of God, making the Word of God alive—something divine. *"Our sufficiency is from God, who also made us sufficient as ministers of the...Spirit; for the...Spirit gives life"* (2 Corinthians 3:5–6).

I knew a believer whose job was to carry bags of coal. He had been in bed for three weeks, away from his work. I showed him Romans 7:25: *"I thank God; through Jesus Christ our Lord! So then, with the mind I myself serve the law of God, but with the flesh the law of sin."* I said, "Keep your mind on God and go to work, shouting victory." He did, and the first day he was able to carry a hundred bags, his mind stayed on God and kept in peace.

Great peace have those who love Your law, and nothing causes them to
stumble. (Psalm 119:165)

Peace I leave with you, My peace I give to you; not as the world gives do
I give to you. Let not your heart be troubled, neither let it be afraid.
(John 14:27)

You cannot have the knowledge of the Lord without peace and joy. Rejoice in the knowledge of Him. Faith is peace. Not long petitions but faith is peace. Where faith is undisturbed, there is peace. I am speaking of eternal faith, daring to believe what God has said. If I dare to trust Him, I find that what He has said always comes to pass.

If your peace is disturbed, there is something wrong. Apply the blood of Jesus and keep your mind stayed upon Jehovah, where "hearts are fully blessed, finding as He promised, perfect peace and rest." Keep your mind on God, gaining strength in Him day by day.

"The law was given through Moses, but grace and truth came through Jesus Christ" (John 1:17). This is a new dispensation, this divine place: Christ in you, the hope and evidence of glory (Colossians 1:27).

May God gird you with truth (Ephesians 6:14). I commend you to Him in the name of Jesus.

Thought for today: If you are not free in the Holy Spirit, your mind is in the wrong place.

THE PLAN OF THE SPIRIT

[God] raised us up together, and made us sit together in
the heavenly places in Christ Jesus.
—Ephesians 2:6

Scripture reading: Luke 10:1–18

It has been a long time now since the debt of sin was settled, our redemption was secured, and death was abolished. Mortality is a hindrance, but death no longer has power. Sin no longer has dominion. You reign in Christ; you take hold of His finished work.

Don't groan and travail for a week if you are in need; *"only believe"* (Mark 5:36). Don't fight to get some special thing; *"only believe."* It is according to your faith that you will receive (Matthew 9:29). God blesses you with faith. *"Have faith in God"* (Mark 11:22). If you are free in God, believe, and it will come to pass.

The work is done if you only believe it. It is done. *"He Himself took our infirmities and bore our sicknesses"* (Matthew 8:17). If only you can see the Lamb of God going to Calvary! He took our flesh so that He could take upon Himself the full burden of all our sin and all the consequences of sin. Then He was raised, so that we might be raised with Him. *"If then you were raised with Christ, seek those things which are above, where Christ is, sitting at the right hand of God"* (Colossians 3:1).

If only you will see Him as God's Lamb, as God's beloved Son, upon whom was laid *"the iniquity of us all"* (Isaiah 53:6). If only you will see that Jesus paid the whole price for our redemption so that we might be free. Then you can enter into your purchased inheritance of salvation, of life, and of power.

Stir yourselves up, beloved! Where are you? I have been planted with Christ in the likeness of His death, and I am risen with Christ (Romans 6:5 KJV). It was a beautiful planting. I am seated with Him in heavenly places (Ephesians 2:6). God credits me with righteousness through faith in Christ (Romans 4:5), and I believe Him. Why should I doubt? Why do you doubt? Faith reigns. God makes it possible.

How many receive the Holy Spirit, and Satan gets a doubt in? Don't doubt; believe. There is power and strength in Him. Who will dare to believe God? Leave Doubting Street; live on Faith-Victory Street. Jesus sent the seventy out, and they came back in victory (Luke 10:1–18). It takes God to make it real.

Thought for today: Dare to believe until there is not a sick person, until everything that is not of God is withered, and the life of Jesus is implanted within.

FILLED TO THE UTMOST

He who believes in Me, as the Scripture has said, out of his heart will
flow rivers of living water. But this He spoke concerning the Spirit,
whom those believing in Him would receive.
—John 7:38–39

Scripture reading: John 7:37–40

In one place in ministry, I stayed in rooms on a side street. I arrived at 9:30 in the morning, but the meeting wasn't until 4:30, so I went to the coast for a few hours of rest.

When I came back to my rooms, the street was full from one end to the other with wheelchairs and cars filled with the helpless and needy. The ministry leaders asked, "What are we going to do?" I answered, "The Holy Spirit came to abide, to reign in supreme royal dignity. Live in freedom, anointing, inspiration, like a river flowing. Settle for nothing less, so that God may be glorified."

God loosed the people and brought healing and deliverance to the captives. Was that all? No, it was only the beginning! The house was packed, too!

Oh, the joy of being ready! God must set us all on fire. There is much land to be possessed. The fields are ripe for harvest (John 4:35).

Oh, the cry of the people! Talk about weeping! Oh, the joy of weeping. You are in an awful place when you cannot weep when the breath of God is upon you. I continued helping the people.

Oh, the breath of the Spirit! Jesus said, *"The Spirit of the Lord is upon Me"* (Luke 4:18). God spoke to me as clearly as could be, saying, "Ask Me! I'll give you all in the place." I thought this was something too big, but He whispered again, "Ask; I will give you all in the house." I said, "Oh, my God, say it again." "Ask of Me. I will give you all in the house." I cried, "I ask! I ask in faith! I believe it!" The breath of heaven filled the place. The people continued to fall down, weeping, crying, repenting.

There is something wonderful in this breath of heaven. Jesus said, "*The Spirit of the Lord is upon Me.*" I repeat, "*Upon Me!*" May God move our hearts to act in this anointing.

Do you want God to have you in His splendid place? Is it the longing of your heart to come to this place? God can choose only those filled to the utmost. How many long to step into line, filled to the utmost, hungering and thirsting after God's fullness? Stand in a living experience as Jesus did, saying, "*The Spirit of the Lord is upon* [me]." May God grant it to every one of you.

Thought for today: Be filled with the Holy Spirit and walk in the Spirit's power.

GOD'S TRANSFORMING POWER

*Therefore, if anyone is in Christ, he is a new creation; old things have
passed away; behold, all things have become new.*
—2 Corinthians 5:17

Scripture reading: 2 Corinthians 5:12–20

The Scriptures do not tell two different stories. They tell the truth. I want
you to know the truth, *"and the truth shall make you free"* (John 8:32). What
is truth? Jesus said, *"I am the way, the truth, and the life"* (John 14:6). He also
said, *"He who believes in Me, as the Scripture has said, out of his heart will
flow rivers of living water"* (John 7:38). He said this concerning the Holy
Spirit, who would be given after Jesus had been glorified (v. 39).

I find nothing in the Bible but holiness, and nothing in the world but
worldliness. Therefore, if I live in the world, I will become worldly; on the
other hand, if I live in the Bible, I will become holy. This is the truth, *"and
the truth shall make you free"* (John 8:32).

The power of God can remodel you. He can make you hate sin and love
righteousness (Psalm 45:7). He can take away bitterness and hatred and
covetousness and malice. He can so consecrate you by His power, through
His blood, that you are made pure and every bit holy—pure in mind, heart,
and actions, pure right through.

God has given me the way of life, and I want to faithfully give it to you,
as though this were the last day I had to live. Jesus is the best blessing, and
you can take Him away with you this morning. God gave His Son to be *"the
propitiation for [y]our sins, and not for [y]ours only but also for the whole world"*
(1 John 2:2).

Jesus came to make us free from sin—free from disease and pain.
When I see a person diseased and in pain, I have great compassion for him.

When I lay my hands upon him, I know God intends for men to be so filled with Him that the power of sin has no effect on them. He intends for them to go forth, as I am doing, to help the needy, sick, and afflicted.

But what is the main thing? To preach *"the kingdom of God and His righteousness"* (Matthew 6:33). Jesus came to do this. John also came preaching repentance (Mark 1:4). The disciples began by preaching *"repentance toward God and faith toward our Lord Jesus Christ"* (Acts 20:21). I tell you, beloved, if you have really been changed by God, there is a repentance in your heart that you will never regret having there.

Through the revelation of the Word of God, we find that divine healing is solely for the glory of God. Moreover, salvation is to make you know that now you are inhabited by another, even God, and that now you are to walk with God *"in newness of life"* (Romans 6:4).

Thought for today: When the Spirit of God comes into your body, He transforms you; He gives you life!

ABOUT THE AUTHOR

An encounter with Smith Wigglesworth (1859–1947) was an unforgettable experience. This seems to be the universal reaction of all who knew him or heard him speak. Smith Wigglesworth was a simple yet remarkable man who was used in an extraordinary way by our extraordinary God. He had a contagious and inspiring faith. Under his ministry, thousands of people came to salvation, committed themselves to a deeper faith in Christ, received the baptism in the Holy Spirit, and were miraculously healed. The power that brought these kinds of results was the presence of the Holy Spirit, who filled Smith Wigglesworth and used him in bringing the good news of the Gospel to people all over the world. Wigglesworth gave glory to God for everything that was accomplished through his ministry, and he wanted people to understand his work only in this context, because his sole desire was that people would see Jesus and not himself.

Smith Wigglesworth was born in England in 1859. Immediately after his conversion as a boy, he had a concern for the salvation of others and won people to Christ, including his mother. Even so, as a young man, he could not express himself well enough to give a testimony in church, much less preach a sermon. Wigglesworth said that his mother had the same difficulty in expressing herself that he did. This family trait, coupled with the fact that he had no formal education because he began working twelve hours a day at the age of seven to help support the family, contributed to Wigglesworth's awkward speaking style. He became a plumber by trade, yet he continued to devote himself to winning many people to Christ on an individual basis.

In 1882, he married Polly Featherstone, a vivacious young woman who loved God and had a gift of preaching and evangelism. It was she who taught him to read and who became his closest confidant and strongest supporter.

They both had compassion for the poor and needy in their community, and they opened a mission, at which Polly preached. Significantly, people were miraculously healed when Wigglesworth prayed for them.

In 1907, Wigglesworth's circumstances changed dramatically when, at the age of forty-eight, he was baptized in the Holy Spirit. Suddenly, he had a new power that enabled him to preach, and even his wife was amazed at the transformation. This was the beginning of what became a worldwide evangelistic and healing ministry that reached thousands. He eventually ministered in the United States, Australia, South Africa, and all over Europe. His ministry extended up to the time of his death in 1947.

Several emphases in Smith Wigglesworth's life and ministry characterize him: a genuine, deep compassion for the unsaved and sick; an unflinching belief in the Word of God; a desire that Christ should increase and he should decrease (John 3:30); a belief that he was called to exhort people to enlarge their faith and trust in God; an emphasis on the baptism in the Holy Spirit with the manifestation of the gifts of the Spirit as in the early church; and a belief in complete healing for everyone of all sickness.

Smith Wigglesworth was called "The Apostle of Faith" because absolute trust in God was a constant theme of both his life and his messages. In his meetings, he would quote passages from the Word of God and lead lively singing to help build people's faith and encourage them to act on it. He emphasized belief in the fact that God could do the impossible. He had great faith in what God could do, and God did great things through him.

Welcome to Our House!

We Have a Special Gift for You ...

It is our privilege and pleasure to share in your love of Christian classics by publishing books that enrich your life and encourage your faith.

To show our appreciation, we invite you to sign up to receive a specially selected **Reader Appreciation Gift**, with our compliments. Just go to the Web address at the bottom of this page.

God bless you as you seek a deeper walk with Him!

WE HAVE A GIFT FOR YOU

whpub.me/classicthx

WHITAKER
HOUSE